MW00476411

THE PEOPLE PILL

THE CURE *for* EVERY MANAGER'S NUMBER ONE PROBLEM

KEN WRIGHT

Amanda Gore International

Published by Amanda Gore Pty Ltd
ACN 088 184 810 trading in the United States
as Amanda Gore International
C/- PACA
Suite 3, Level 8, North Tower
1-5 Railway Street, Chatswood
NSW 2067 AUSTRALIA
61 2 9415 4877

Distributed by Greenleaf Book Group LLC

For ordering information or special discounts for bulk purchases, please contact Greenleaf Book Group LLC at 4425 S. Mo Pac Expy., Suite 600, Austin, TX 78735, (512) 891-6100.

Design and composition by Greenleaf Book Group LLC
Cover design by Greenleaf Book Group LLC

ISBN: 978-0-9818794-0-6

Publisher's Cataloging-in-Publication Data
(Prepared by The Donohue Group, Inc.)

Wright, Ken (Kenneth Leslie), 1949-
   The people pill : the cure for every manager's number one problem /
Ken Wright. -- 1st ed.

   p. ; cm.

   Includes bibliographical references.
   ISBN: 978-0-9818794-0-6

1. Personnel management. 2. Leadership. I. Title.

HF5549 .W754 2008
658.3   2008930811

Printed in the United States of America on acid-free paper

13 12 11 10 09   10 9 8 7 6 5 4 3 2

First Edition

CONTENTS

What Business Leaders Are Saying About *The People Pill*

"*The People Pill* is exactly what every manager needs. It's honest, practical, enlightening, and puts the responsibility for a problem-free workplace where it belongs—on leaders."
—Vanessa Castagna, former CEO, JCPenney Stores, Catalog, Internet

"Do not read this book if you want to learn to manage. Read this book and read it again if you want to lead."
—Vince Poscente, *New York Times* best-selling author of *The Age of Speed*

"Leadership is as much art as it is science, and Ken Wright knows both intimately. *The People Pill* is a must read for anyone who plays a leadership role, no matter how much or how little experience you've had as a leader. Both insightful and educational, it's a great addition to your library of leadership know how!"
—Peter Hearl, chief operating and development officer, YUM Brands, Inc.

"Ken Wright has written a fabulous book that very simply tells others how to lead their teams by building connections with people. I've personally worked with Ken and have seen him lead his team to great results by connecting to their hearts. It is a must for all leaders who want to build successful teams."
—John Symond AM, founder and CEO, Aussie Home Loans

PREFACE

THIS IS NOT a typical business advice book, exploring a single "silver bullet" idea that can totally eliminate all of your people problems. It is a practical, simple guide grounded in the basic element of success with people—being an authentic leader who understands what it takes to get the best results from individuals and a team. The methods in this book are hard-tested adaptations of the techniques I've personally seen produce great results over the past twenty-five years.

To provide more context for the stories I use to ground the principles and tools presented in the book, I need to first offer some personal history. I am the son of a butcher and a seamstress, raised in Horsham, Australia. As both a shop owner and landlord, my father displayed a generous nature. For example, when I spent time in the shop, I would often watch him "slip in" steaks or chops for poorer customers who had asked for the very cheapest cuts of meat. And when triplets were born to a family of renters who were forced to consider moving out of the home they rented from my parents, my father allowed them to live rent-free for nine months so they could recover from their financial strain and eventually meet their rent obligation. My mother also exhibited a sense of generosity in her work as a seamstress, giving away many of the clothes she made to less fortunate people in our community.

My father knew that his openhandedness ultimately paid dividends and always said that the "extras" he provided would certainly generate more business through word of mouth. And he believed that treating staff and customers—in fact, all people—with fairness and generosity was good for the soul as well as good for business. My firm commitment to the now-popular concept of "wowing the customer" originated, for me, in my father's interpretation of the Horsham area's annual celebration, WOW week, which was actually named for the core resources of wheat, oats, and wool. My father converted the acronym to suit his business philosophy.

The wow factor was the core of his customer service philosophy. He even had a wow budget, and he explained the importance of this approach as the law of reciprocity—you give first and receive second.

I recall him telling me about the four points of good business:

❶ Build relationships.

❷ Be great at what you do and offer excellent products and service.

❸ Deliver what you promise—always.

❹ Find a way to wow them, and they will never forget you.

At the ripe age of thirteen, I began putting his principles into practice with customers on my morning and evening paper routes. On cold, wet mornings, I delivered papers to my customers' verandas (often along with their delivered milk) so they would not have to brave the elements. After all, I was already cold and wet! I also sent Christmas cards to customers a week before the holiday. Other paperboys marveled at the generosity of my customers when I received tips three to four times what they received, but I knew I had earned those tips through excellent service. I wowed my customers, knowing it paid off for me in the long run.

At that age, I had already learned valuable lessons about how to succeed. But forming the intentions and finding the focus to make that success happen took a bit longer. My true youthful passion was sports—almost any sport. And at the age of sixteen, I left school and began working at a bank as a junior postage clerk, believing it was a short-term role while I pursued my dream of becoming a professional athlete. But that dream never came to fruition. Had I focused intently on a single sport, I may have developed into the professional athlete I aspired to be. What I lacked was not attitude or ability, but a clear goal that combined the resources of my head and my heart.

By age eighteen I had reevaluated my goal of a career in sports and decided to marshal my resources, develop a clear goal, and execute a plan to achieve it. I set a goal of becoming one of five state managers for the bank, which had more than forty thousand employees. Achieving this goal would require strength of conviction (others saw the goal as a long shot), the ability to identify the obstacles I would have to clear, and a plan for negotiating the many stepping-stones along the way—it would take a strong heart, a clear head, and the will to execute. At age twenty-nine, when a merger created the Australian bank Westpac, I became the youngest manager in that organization—a product of using all of my resources to advance and learn along the way. I had become a voracious consumer of all available training material, made a habit of finishing my own tasks quickly, and always reached out to help others.

At this time in my career, I was already aware of the impact of a leader's emotional style and that leaders have one role that is more important than any other: connecting with and developing people, creating an environment where people enjoy coming to work. I knew that a great leader needs to inspire the spirit in people, ignite it, and keep the flame fueled. It was evident to me that if you want to change an organization, you have to lead a change of heart. A leader who has his head and heart connected can authentically lead a team to develop the essential relationships to achieve amazing results. These relationship-building skills can create a dynamic network among staff, business partners, and customers that will drive the business.

When I was thirty-six, new events pushed me to form an altogether new goal. A visiting state manager had told me to "cool my heels" while my future career path with the bank took shape. I decided to go after a different opportunity by resigning my bank position after twenty years to join the newly formed insurance division, Westpac Life—but as a salesperson, not a manager. I knew that my people skills would shine through, leading me to success as a salesperson and to greater leadership opportunities. Despite being entirely new to the insurance business, I was the third top salesperson in an Australian sales force of more than four hundred that first year. Six years later, I became CEO, with the authority to apply the principles and methods I'd learned through the years—all centered on people, making them feel important and developing their skills to deliver outstanding service and to produce excellent results.

What my experience as a manager and leader has taught me is that there is no more important task than building relationships with people (internally and externally) and helping people develop their own skills. The principles, priorities, methods, and tools I present in the pages that follow really work to engage the hearts and minds of your people. Although many of the ideas are borrowed and adapted, I've worked hard to formulate them into a systematic approach that serves the bottom line and develops mutual respect between people. Applying these ideas has produced great results for me and the people around me: in six years as CEO at Westpac Investments & Insurance, I led the organization to increase profitability by more than 400 percent and to dramatically increase customer and staff satisfaction to a consistent 97 or 98 percent. The key to obtaining these great results was having a team of leaders truly operating from the heart, with a passionate desire to really care about their people, engage them, and develop them to their full potential.

The Institute of HeartMath has been conducting scientific research on the role that leading from the heart can play in dramatically improving employee performance and well-being. The key to engaging people is a heart-to-heart connection that makes them feel they are cared for. The institute clarifies the essence of its work in a psychological equation: "activating heart intelligence + managing the mind + managing the emotions = energy efficiency, increased coherence, enhanced awareness, and greater productivity" (Childre, Martin, & Beech, 1999). Many leaders try to turn business into a purely logical exercise. They focus on the bottom line and are proud to call themselves "results driven." For guidance and direction, they look at numbers. But where do growth and profit really come from? From the employees that are responsible for the numbers and the customers they serve. If your employees and customers are unhappy, the bottom line will be a disaster.

Your commitment to better people skills, to better relationships, is a path to realizing your own full potential. When you are successful in applying both your head and your heart to the relationships that drive your business, you will get noticed as a leader. New opportunities will unfold, and your professional horizons will expand. And that's what I hope this book will bring you.

ACKNOWLEDGMENTS

I OWE A special debt of gratitude to my wife, Amanda Gore. Without her insistence that I have some unique methods of leading and developing people and a great story to tell, this book would never have come into being.

There are three people who are no longer with us who also contributed to the book. My father and mother, Les and Clytie Wright, were, and still are, generous souls. Until I was writing this book, I did not truly understand or appreciate how much of my business philosophy was learned in my early years observing and listening to my father. He passed away when I was 18, when I thought that I knew everything and that he wasn't cool! Amanda's mum, Lenore Gore, was extraordinary. Mama had a tough life, but was continually focused on the positives. She built me up more than anyone—thanks Mama for your love and support.

To the people that I have worked with over my career, you have created many opportunities to learn—what to do and what not to do! I have had the pleasure to work in and lead some great teams, producing excellent results and having lots of fun. Two people I've worked with, Tony Monaco and Spiros Christoforatos, encouraged me to write the book and made significant contributions. Inspiring leaders I've worked with—David Cheatley, Bob Joss, David Liddy, John Symond, James Symond, and my mentor Drew Tanzman—have all helped me develop the insights and skills necessary to be a successful leader.

Robert and Cheryl Sardello from the School of Spiritual Psychology deserve a special mention for their contribution in developing my heart capacities, which are now clearly reflected in all I do.

Kirk Palmer for his great work in helping me pull the initial manuscript into shape.

The proofreading, suggestions, and ideas in the early stages by Roxie Banker, Peter Hearl, Somer McCormick, Jay Morris, and Vince Poscente, and the research, ideas, and edits from Denise Rizzo, were most appreciated.

To my editors, Lari Bishop, Jay Hodges, and Erin Nelsen: You were a delight to work with and brought forth constructive criticism and many excellent new ideas!

Finally to my children, Matt, Rebecca, and Renee: You have supported my endeavors at all times and have given me many proud moments—and on a number of occasions the opportunity to develop my leadership skills.

INTRODUCTION

WHY IS ENGAGING people, particularly employees, so difficult? We've all heard the sayings "If it wasn't for the customers, this business would be great" and "If I didn't have to deal with employees, this business would be enjoyable." These statements are almost always made tongue in cheek, but there is some truth in them. The reason they feel true to many leaders is that most leaders do not understand how to connect with and engage their people, how to build relationships that are mutually beneficial and that result in positive outcomes. In short, they don't know how to be great leaders.

Consider the following statements (statistics from Gallup Organization and TNS Media Intelligence):

- **Four out of ten American employees feel disconnected with their employers. (TNS Media Intelligence)**
- **Disengaged workers cost the U.S. economy $328 billion. (Gallup)**
- **A meager 18 percent of Australians believe they are engaged at work. (Gallup)**
- **Disengaged workers aren't just unhappy at work—every day these people undermine what their engaged coworkers accomplish. (Gallup)**
- **Only 33 percent of American employees view their managers as strong leaders. (TNS Media Intelligence)**
- **As many as 90 percent of Americans leave their jobs when they fail to make an emotional connection with their boss. (Gallup)**

Companies that do not have these people issues have leaders who can cultivate and leverage positive relationships with their people and their customers, relationships that foster trust, consideration, and mutual benefit. They truly connect with people, engage them, and create environments that promote high morale and motivation, consistent recognition, initiative and collaboration, and the highest levels of performance.

I believe that when employees fail, and eventually companies fail, it's due to one or more of these factors:

- Poor selection at hiring time—our selection
- Poor skills left undeveloped—our coaching and development
- Poor attitude allowed to persist—our environment
- Poor leadership—our abilities

All four reasons have one very big thing in common—us. As leaders, we have the power and influence to prevent the great majority of these failures.

In my experience, the best way to create soaring profits and long-term success is to focus on people and work closely with them to bring out their full potential. When we recognize the true connection between people's overall well-being and their work performance, we understand the importance of leading from both the head and the heart. People become more productive, teams more cohesive, and customers more satisfied. This isn't magic or mysticism. I offer seven simple prescriptions to help you.

❶ Earn the respect and trust of your employees.

❷ Create a highly energized and positive workplace, resulting in the high morale and productivity that is essential to excellent, long-term financial results.

❸ Keep your most valued employees content and loyal.

❹ Deal with performance issues efficiently and effectively.

❺ Focus everybody on delivering excellent customer service.

❻ Create buy-in and dedication to the company's strategic goals.

❼ Develop your personal leadership skills.

🧪 Lab Work

A survey of 1,500 employees in January 2007 by Ros Taylor Ltd. found that 77 percent claim their supervisor is not interested in them; 79 percent indicate that their managers do not set clear goals; 90 percent think their boss does nothing about poor performance; and 89 percent say their supervisor is not receptive to new ideas and lacks innovation (Taylor, 2007). Don't be a toxic leader; reach out to your employees in various ways.

Once you grasp the principles and techniques that can truly impact results, you are positioned to build a successful team and organization—and de-stress your day. Studying and absorbing the seven prescriptions I present, implementing them without fail and without taking shortcuts, adapting them as necessary to your specific business and values along the way: these are the keys to success.

PRESCRIPTION 1

THE CURE FOR EMPLOYEES
WHO DON'T RESPECT YOU

IN ALMOST ANY relationship, people want to be respected. That desire becomes a necessity for people in managerial roles. Without the respect of your team, how will you achieve great results? It will be almost impossible.

Many leaders who don't have the respect of their team blame this lack of respect usually either on their team's poor attitude and unwillingness to follow direction or on the company leaders' poor direction. But an employee's respect for a leader is based on two elements: trust in the leader and feeling valued by the leader. Without these elements, even managers who are skilled at what they do will have a hard time earning the respect of their teams and leveraging that respect to take their team to a higher level of performance.

The first prescription I'm offering is:

 If you want to earn the respect of your team, earn their trust and show them that you value them as people and employees.

BUILD TRUST

It is critical in any relationship to have trust. Whether it's among the members on a sports team, among members of a family, or between a manager and an employee in an office, trust is the glue that holds people together. In any situation, a lack of trust means there is going to be trouble. In the office, if employees don't trust their manager, then they will view all his decisions with suspicion. When a manager's motives are in question, employees will be slower to accept any change, no matter how positive that change appears on the surface.

How do successful managers earn the trust of their employees? By behaving in trustworthy ways and constantly exhibiting character and integrity, they convey honesty, fairness, and consistency. The process of "climbing the ladder" can destroy a manager's humility. Don't let that happen to you. Remain in touch with your people and your own heart, and you'll find the trust and respect you're seeking.

Leadership is about making tough decisions. A leader has to prioritize results, identify workable strategies and plans, and incorporate the reality of every challenge and obstacle. And if you want your employees to trust you, these decisions must seem honest, fair, and consistent. Many leaders shy away from "courageous conversations" because they fall into the trap of wanting to be liked. But

🧪 Lab Work

A 2005 Watson Wyatt WorkUSA survey found that companies with high integrity—measured by employee assessments of senior management's consistency, communications, and other trust-determining behaviors—generate financial returns that are twice those of companies with low integrity levels ("Companywide Trust Affects Productivity, Profitability," Krell, 2006).

The same study found that 72 percent of employees believe their immediate bosses act with honesty and integrity in their business activities, but only 56 percent believe that about top management (Krell, 2006).

Communication World conveyed similar findings from Watson Wyatt studies done in the United States and the United Kingdom, and from MORI, an independent research company in the United Kingdom. The Watson Wyatt study indicated that most employees do not trust senior executives. But MORI reported that employees viewed their immediate manager as a trusted source for delivering accurate company information (Larkan & Larkin, 2006).

being courageous about tackling tough issues builds respect, and the good performers in your team will admire this strong leadership.

I recommend consulting the following checklist when you're considering a decision:

- ✔ Is my decision as fair as possible to all concerned?
- ✔ Does my decision violate the law, or my company's vision and values?

✔ Have I applied my heart as well as my head in looking at this decision?

✔ Would I make the same decision if I knew my action would make the six o'clock news?

As a leader, you are intent on succeeding. But the success worth achieving is success you can feel good about—in your heart, as well as intellectually. Although that doesn't resolve all our challenges, it provides a useful guideline. My life in business has convinced me beyond a doubt that we don't have to choose between success and a clear conscience. And if we want to build trust, we had better not ask others to make that kind of choice either. Of course, building trust involves more than just doing the right thing. It also means making sure you can follow through with other aspects of earning respect.

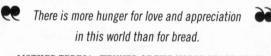

There is more hunger for love and appreciation in this world than for bread.

—MOTHER TERESA, WINNER OF THE NOBEL PEACE PRIZE

Be Approachable

The more approachable you are the more trust you will gain among your employees and colleagues. Everyone wants to work with people they trust and feel comfortable around. That comfort level comes from openness and honesty. Are you open with your team and colleagues?

To find out if the people you work with view you as approachable, just ask them. Ask your employees if they feel comfortable coming to you with concerns and issues. Ask your colleagues if they feel comfortable confiding in you. Find out from your superiors if they view you as approachable. Constantly monitor your openness.

One way to exhibit openness is to ask for feedback—and take it to heart. If you don't already have a system for this, develop one. Make sure your team members know that you can handle constructive criticism—and you want it. Then use this feedback for your own constant improvement—the same constant improvement you demand from them. If you find that you are not receiving feedback on ways to improve your leadership style or business processes, conduct an anonymous survey aimed at finding out the real picture. If this elicits the constructive criticism that no one would give you before, look closely at your leadership style. Ask yourself, what am I projecting that makes people feel that they cannot be open and honest with me?

Being more open and approachable is a valuable and admirable aspiration, and it helps build trust. But one word of caution: don't lose your leadership perspective. Stay upright and focused on the organization's goals. You must balance the interests of employees, customers, and shareholders if you want to succeed as a leader.

VALUE PEOPLE

Making people feel valued is one of the most important roles of an authentic leader. To take this step toward being a better leader and earning the respect of your employees, you must connect with them on both an intellectual and an emotional level, and you must exhibit a true commitment to developing their knowledge and skills.

True coaching, targeted at developing the whole person, comes from the heart, and every technique I'll share in this section passes the same important test. Each is an authentic, respectful, and empathetic means of driving toward improved performance.

Connect with Employees

People feel valued when they know their leader has taken the time and put in the effort to really connect with them.

Connecting is all about discovering the needs of the people you are trying to develop, and putting your heart into doing what is best for them. When they *feel* you doing this authentically, their trust in you goes up and their loyalty to the company rises as well.

UNDERSTANDING AND CONNECTING with her people must be a manager's number-one priority. It's more important than the numbers for any given month, and more important than enforcing any one policy or procedure. Making this connection requires *truly* getting to know your people. You must empathize with their individual needs to conquer challenges, to feel supported, and to be valued.

This is critical: the best decisions can only come from knowing your people, connecting with them at a heart level, and working with them to develop their skills. You need to know your people and your business more thoroughly and intimately than anyone else. Your decisions will be respected and deliver results *only if* you connect with your people on an emotional level as well as intellectually. This level of connection enables both trust and respect and will help you know what skills each person can develop and how. In turn, trust and respect allow you to be open and objective as you work to develop your people.

The aim of the great leader is not to get people to think more highly
of the leader. It's to get people to think more highly of themselves.

—EDGE LEARNING

If your people feel that you know them and care about them, that will have a fantastic impact on performance. People happy in their roles, carrying a strong sense of purpose, will perform exceptionally. Such a wave of clear intention and healthy self-esteem is the best way to drive results from any sales team.

Be Visible

One route to connecting with people that is key to making employees feel valued is a manager's visibility. Respect for you, across your organization, will increase tenfold if people see you frequently spending time "on the floor," at the ground level. You need to resonate with your people on every level, showing them that you truly understand the challenges they face. Personally, I've taken this commitment to the level of insisting to be included on the kitchen-duty list. Where I've seen a spill, I've cleaned it up—even as CEO.

The power a leader gains from visibility and participation is amazing. You are highly visible and constantly scrutinized anyway, so rise to the challenge of showing your people that they are highly valued by displaying your feelings and conveying a sincere desire to connect with them personally and professionally. Every interaction with your people should be treated as a great opportunity to reinforce vision, values, and expectations, as you build their self-esteem. The results for all will be awesome!

Encourage Personal Growth

Think about this important distinction: Managers manage things; leaders develop people.

You've probably heard it before and it may seem like a cliché. But it's frequently quoted because it rings true—if we recognize that our real gains and successes as leaders come from helping others reach their potential.

Developing people is the single most important job of any leader. I'm absolutely certain of that. This subject hits me right in the heart, because it's where I get my greatest "buzz" and take my greatest satisfaction. My own success has come out of my passion for seeing people grow to be the best they can be. I love seeing them reach and exceed their potential—as leaders, sales representatives, professionals in other roles, yes, but also as confident, fulfilled people, whom you have really connected with and have helped to achieve their dreams. That fantastic buzz comes from seeing people develop their skills, attitudes, and self-esteem beyond what even they thought possible.

When thinking about developing people, it's helpful to remember the acronym KASH:

- **Knowledge:** The committed employee will want to be continually learning. Facilitate this desire by working closely with your employees on their own personal development plans (see page 22).

- **Attitude:** By creating a positive culture focused on development, attitude will improve (see Prescription 2).

- **Skills:** Work on a skills improvement with every employee on a monthly basis with the goal of improving by at least 10 percent.

- **Habits:** Encourage all your leaders to set a good example. Good habits will thrive in your organization if an excellent example is set from the top.

At the root of my philosophy is a very simple principle. It's much more beneficial *and cost-effective* to develop people—and make a strong effort to rehabilitate them when they underachieve—than to have a "revolving door" on your team. When a team member fails and must be replaced, the costs are tremendous. Develop and improve the KASH of your people and watch your business reap the cash. Avoiding those costs by committing to development does require huge effort, however. Most important is a passionate commitment to

- an intensive, disciplined hiring process that enables a solid evaluation of attitude and soft skills, as well as hard skills and experience;
- a method for developing all the skills our people need to succeed;
- a positive environment where coaching and growth are truly valued; and
- an authentic, connected way of leading by providing frequent, honest feedback and investing in rehabilitation when needed.

We will deal extensively with employee recruitment, selection, and retention in another prescription. For now, let's just recognize that our processes for finding the right people will be thorough and consistent. This is an incredibly important part of creating a true "people development" culture of success. It provides the base for knowing that our efforts with our people are justified, because we have every reason to believe they are capable of delivering what we expect: excellent performance.

In his book *Inspire! What Great Leaders Do* (2004), leadership thinker and pioneer Lance Secretan succinctly states the importance of employee development.

> Unless I am vigilant, I will become a prisoner of process instead of an enjoyer of experience. How much of our time is spent on the means rather than the ends—the rules and policies, the structures (strategic plans, budgets, proposals, compensation programs, agendas, etc.), and the rituals (meetings, voice mail, email, performance appraisals, agendas, and politics)?
>
> Thinking about this question can help us refocus on our most important activity: developing our people in ways that promote success.

SEVEN CRITICAL PEOPLE RULES TO LIVE BY

A leader's ultimate challenges are building a team intently focused on delivering exceptional results and delivering real, recognizable value for customers and shareholders while creating and sustaining a culture that values people and rewards results.

The common thread between these goals is a true commitment to building relationships and connecting with and developing people. To help you infuse this commitment into your actions and your organization, I've developed seven guidelines. These are rules to live by. Practicing them with everyone on your team is essential to earning the respect of your team. If they believe in you as a connected leader, they will trust you, respect you, perform excellently, and have the right attitude to work hard for improvement.

❶ **Listen without judging.** Encourage open and honest feedback between yourself and all of your people. Determine what they want to get out of the job: What are their goals? What do they need? What obstacles are they facing? Approach each topic or concern by really listening with your heart, without judgment. You must encourage your people to share their needs, dreams, and obstacles with you. You need open, honest discussion and feedback to help them achieve excellence.

❷ **Empathize and show compassion.** Spend time with each of your people and find out what is happening in their lives, not only at work but in their personal lives as well. Empathy is the ability to actually feel the pain or joy of another person. Empathy helps you understand someone else's position, and it's the first step to showing compassion. I see compassion as "the commitment to connect with passion."

Whenever your employees make the effort to share feelings, concerns, suggestions, or constructive criticism, you need to show you care. By taking a true interest in your staff, you will relay to them that your company cares not only about its bottom line but also about each individual working there.

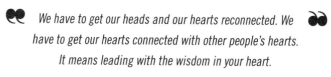

We have to get our heads and our hearts reconnected. We have to get our hearts connected with other people's hearts. It means leading with the wisdom in your heart.

—AMANDA GORE, MOTIVATIONAL SPEAKER AND CONNECTION EXPERT

❸ **Be authentic.** Reflect often on your goals for people, making sure they come from your heartfelt desire to improve your employees' skills and their lives. Understand that people need to feel challenged and believe that their work adds value. By respecting your employees as people (and not simply as a means to increase revenue), you will gain their respect. They will genuinely work harder because they believe in the work that they are doing and in you as a leader. This can absolutely be compatible with your desire to improve results.

❹ **Give honest feedback.** You need to always be fair and polite, looking first to be a "good finder." This means searching for the good in people and recognizing it—out loud. Show them what they are doing well and give them some suggestions about how they can improve. Then follow up. Commend them for taking your advice. If they are still falling short, point out the problem and ask them to come up with a solution. When you put the ball in their court, they will realize you trust them and value their opinions, and consequently they will work harder to maintain that trust. When you must be critical, check your motives and test yourself for fairness. Remember Rule 2: Empathize and show compassion when providing constructive criticism. Any corrective feedback carries an emotional charge, so the way it is delivered is as important as the accuracy and fairness of the critique itself.

❺ **Share your knowledge and vision.** Help your people understand the overall strategic goal for your company and how each of their individual roles helps to achieve this vision. Be sure they understand your industry, and educate them on issues, changes, and advances in the industry as well. Not only will your people appreciate you taking the time to educate them, they will also have a better understanding why and when you have to make difficult decisions. They will also be able to make better judgments and decisions if they have all of the information they need. Tell your people what you see happening in your organization and your industry. They will appreciate it, feel valued, and gain confidence in you and the organization.

❻ Provide training. Determine what skills and expertise each employee currently has, and then compare them to the skills and attributes needed to excel in the role. Provide specifically tailored training programs to help move your people toward maximizing their potential. When someone is great at what he does, he is more likely to enjoy it and be actively engaged. This will have a direct effect on productivity, the service your team provides to internal and external customers, and ultimately your bottom line. But you must personally analyze individual needs and follow through with specific training to address those needs.

❼ Consult and plan. In addition to having a vision for your company, you need to have a people plan for the future. While you may have a plan for the business, do you have a personal development plan for each employee? You should. Every person on your team needs to have a specific development plan in place. You then need to get involved in their efforts toward achieving their goals and dreams. Get frequent input from each employee, and continually evolve these plans to better meet their needs. Let them know how you want to expand, what new markets you want to tap, and how you see them growing with you. They will work harder when they see potential for both their own growth and the expansive possibilities of the company.

These guidelines all feed and reinforce your effectiveness as the leader in your people development culture. You can expect your people to be honest, constructive, and empathetic only if you model all these important skills in your own actions. Where you place your focus is where your team will place its focus.

You will need to be persistent, determined, and involved, particularly if this type of culture is far removed from the current culture in your organization. But the hard work will be worth the effort. Forming a culture around developing people will indirectly drive your business results and create a trustful environment. In my experience, following these seven rules and building a culture of development will result in a serious boost in morale, motivation, retention of valuable employees, and bottom-line results. These gains won't happen overnight, but if you consistently drive this culture change, you will see the benefits sooner than you imagine.

PUT THE FOCUS ON DEVELOPMENT

If you are systematic and consistent in putting people development first on your priority list, your entire team will make the same commitment. Leading the creation of such a culture is not easy. You have to start with your direct reports and set the clear expectation that they will cascade your attitude and processes through their teams. The real organizational cultural change occurs when it starts with the CEO and filters through the entire organization. But the size of your team does not matter, nor does it matter if you do not have other leaders as direct reports. You can still initiate the process of developing your people. Keep in mind that people will know when you are truly committed to this kind of culture change, so don't waste time going through the motions if you're not willing to see it through.

To smooth the change, I've developed a straightforward but intensive process for your creation of a people development culture. It starts with a meeting of all your direct reports, focused on understanding their specific goals, aspirations, and dreams. In this meeting, do the following:

❶ Have your team members reach consensus on a "Ten Most Important Skills and Attributes" list for top performance in their roles. For instance, some attributes might include planning, persistence, and focus on results. If you are managing a group of people in diverse roles, there will be some skill areas that are different. But the majority will still be the same: the soft skills like attitude, enthusiasm, passion, and persistence.

❷ Next, have the team assess one another's skills and identify one person within the group as the model for each skill or attribute—the highest-ranked individual in each category on a scale of 1 to 10, by group agreement. You as a leader will need to guide this process and, if possible, ensure that they select different peers for each skill or attribute.

❸ Work your way through the list of attributes and their models, having each of your highest-ranked people explore out loud what they focus on to excel in that area. For example, the group has ranked Bill a 10 in attitude, so Bill must speak for a few minutes on his approach to maintaining a good attitude.

❹ After each role model speaks, direct every person on the team to think about what they've heard and then give themselves a rating in that particular skill or attribute.

❺ Explain that each team member's next step will be to work with you in deciding on one of the ten areas for immediate focus and improvement. The goal will be concise and manageable: for example, improving their selected area by 10 percent in the course of a month will enable them to lift their rating in that area. For instance, they may be working on "positive attitude," aiming to lift their rating from seven to eight. Keep in mind that the key to achieving personal development goals is to avoid BHAGs—big hairy audacious goals, or in other words, goals that are unrealistic. I often use the word *intention* rather than *goal* because I think it highlights the connection between head and heart that makes achievement possible and ultimately rewarding.

6 Ensure that people do not automatically pick a perceived weakness to work on, explaining to them that often taking a strength to a new level is more effective. Dealing with people's weaknesses in knowledge or skill is covered more completely in Prescription 4.

To implement this method and get the best possible results, you will need to guide the process. First, you may need to gently direct the process of identifying your team's ten key skills and attributes. Make certain that key soft skills such as attitude are not overlooked. For example, a well-balanced list for a team of leaders might include the following:

- Authentic leadership
- Attitude
- Passion, energy, and enthusiasm
- Connection skills
- Recruitment/selection/retention
- Planning and strategy development
- Persistence

- People development
- Recognizing/rewarding/motivating
- Focus on results

When those singled out as models speak about their skills, drill down to get stories showing their real habits and practices. Call attention to simple things they do that make them excel in a certain area. This makes improvement feel more achievable for the rest of the group, as others think, "Really? That's all this person does to ensure such great results? Almost anyone could do that, and it's certainly worth a try for me."

In the "self-rating" phase, it's important to explain clearly and authentically that you believe this is essential for improving skills and achieving goals, as individuals and a team. Put special emphasis on a modest goal: 10 percent improvement in one area at a time, per month. Be empathetic by acknowledging that you know self-rating is difficult, but that it's really essential to making the entire process work. You'll likely find that most people rate themselves lower than you would have rated them. Shown on the next page is a sample rating chart that you might want to prepare ahead of time so that people can take notes throughout the meeting.

Finally, assure your people—and show them—that you fully intend to work with them every step of the way on their quest to improve. Build their confidence by pointing out their strengths and explaining that working on a strength might be more effective than working on a weakness that is not limiting them dramatically. Initially, you may want to simply share a few tips or direct them to a good book or article on the area you agree to work on. Note that this is just a method for focusing your organization on development, not a plan for singling out poor performers and bringing them up to a new level. That process is covered later in the book.

Attribute/Skill	Current Rating, 1–10	Notes on How to Improve Rating
Authentic leadership		
Attitude		
Passion, energy, and enthusiasm		
Connection skills		
Recruitment/selection/retention		
Planning and strategy development		
Persistence		
People development		
Recognizing/rewarding/ motivating		
Focus on results		

There is one more critical step that you must take if you want people to be invested in the process and trust in your commitment to it: you must rank yourself in the ten key areas and set a plan of development for yourself, just as you asked others to do. Don't be afraid to show your team members that you created a plan for yourself; let them know they are not alone in needing to improve skills. This will help engender empathy and moral support as you go about your duties as a leader. Here's a tip: When evaluating a weakness in yourself, always approach it as if it belonged to someone else. This will help you maintain objectivity and provide you space to work toward improvement. And remember to also respect and care for yourself when you discover your own vulnerabilities and opportunities for improvement.

The simple act of showing you care about your people improving specific skills can do wonders. Insisting that people think about each of these skills will do even more. Based on my experience, this first session will have amazing, often unexpected results. For example, having your model 10 in "personal presentation" talk briefly about how she exhibits confidence when speaking with a client will cause others to imitate what works for her.

On top of gains in the focus areas for each individual, there are additional benefits to be had from using this method. In one meeting, you can

- show your people that soft skills truly matter in their success;
- turn abstract "qualities" into a set of habits, practices, tools, and tricks available to everyone;
- start overcoming and disarming the greatest obstacle to improvement: the attitude or thought that "I will never be good at that"; and
- help your team members realize how easy it is to improve 10 percent in a specific skill or attribute.

Your own participation and follow-through will be critical. You cannot drop this ball! Make certain that your monthly follow-ups take place, and that each engagement is sincere and productive. Be sure that the focus is not only on improving the results of the team but also on providing each person with an opportunity to develop his abilities to further his career and achieve his goals. This will help you secure total buy-in.

 Far and away the best prize that life offers is the
chance to work hard at work worth doing.
—THEODORE ROOSEVELT

In my experience, it takes about three months to introduce this process and inculcate it into the team's culture before seeing strong results throughout a team. By that time, team members will have seen their own skills improve and seen their peers improving as well.

Along the way, you should devote at least one meeting to discussing what you've done so far. Allow your team to offer feedback and suggestions for making the whole process work even better. Answer their questions honestly, but insist that they follow through with the process religiously.

You will remain the key to getting results all through your team. You must remain focused and keep a hands-on approach until you feel the process has become embedded in your new people development culture, particularly if you are a higher-level leader with leadership teams reporting to you. You should attend as many of the introductory meetings at the next level as possible, and celebrate every success you see or hear about along the way. Never stop following through on this commitment, and you will build a great foundation for achieving truly outstanding results.

TEAM DEVELOPMENT

As you work through the process of developing your people, it is important to also understand that your team has its own development needs, and its own development stages, in addition to those of the individuals who compose it. Developing the people on a team will fast-track team development, but team development takes time, as the individuals learn to trust, rely on, and work with their teammates.

DIAGNOSIS: A CASE OF THE OFF–SITES

Many managers today lead mobile or off-site workforces, so let's look at the major aspects of leading and developing these employees.

■ Make sure your mobile or off-site employees are following the same development process as the rest of your employees.

■ Encourage teamwork by holding meetings when it's possible for all off-site employees to attend, or utilize videoconferencing or telephone conferencing.

■ Help off-site employees feel part of the bigger picture. Request frequent updates and share ideas and initiatives often. Make sure they are on every important email list.

■ Focus on measuring results—quantity and quality of work, meeting deadlines, etc.—as you won't be able to measure the process each employee goes through to get the results.

■ Rewards, incentives, and competitions should still be communicated to off-site employees as a team, even though they aren't all in the same room.

■ Conduct monthly one-on-one meetings with each off-site employee.

■ Discourage overwork in off-site employees. For those who are driven, working from home presents the risk of working all the time. If they fall into this trap eventually they will burn out and become unproductive. Don't call or email them outside of reasonable business hours.

Let's look at the five stages of team development.

- **Stage 1—Guidance:** New teams need guidance and support, but be careful not to stifle them by micromanaging. This will squash the sharing of ideas and initiatives. It is important in this guidance stage that you be seen as an authentic leader, operating from the heart and working to forge a close connection among team members.

- **Stage 2—Challenge:** As the team develops, there will be conflicts as team members strive to be the top performers. Your role is to massage egos, provide encouragement, and keep everyone focused on the team. As you take your team through this stage, be very aware of feelings; display compassion and empathy as you bring people back to the team path.

- **Stage 3—Working together:** This is where you really earn your money as a leader. As the team grows, your coaching duties begin, and the following leader responsibilities become critical:
    - Team meetings
    - Developing each individual's attributes and skills
    - Monthly one-on-ones
    - Group training sessions
    - Teamwork skills
    - Rewarding and recognizing team efforts
    - Rewarding and recognizing personal bests
    - Celebrating successes

- **Stage 4—Obstacles:** Usually teams will go through a stage of conflict where obstacles seem too huge to surmount; these obstacles will come from both within the organization and outside it. Your role is to have the team see these as speed bumps and not brick walls. Occasionally you will need to be a bulldozer for your team. This means standing up for the team and watching out for its best interests. It also means removing internal obstacles. A leader who supports his team by clearing away obstacles that the team can't control builds enormous respect.

- **Stage 5—Maturity:** Once you have shown the team that obstacles can be overcome, the team will really mature and move on to performing at consistently excellent levels. Now is the time to start involving the team in planning and strategizing.

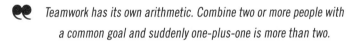

Teamwork has its own arithmetic. Combine two or more people with a common goal and suddenly one-plus-one is more than two.

—DAN ZADRA, AUTHOR OF *TOGETHER WE CAN: CELEBRATING THE POWER OF A TEAM AND A DREAM*

AS YOU SHOULD be able to tell by now, a major focus of this book is investing in people. Certainly when it comes to earning the respect of your team, exhibiting honesty and integrity, connecting with them emotionally and intellectually, and expressing a sincere commitment to helping them develop to improve their personal success and the success of the team are the most critical steps. These elements are the foundational skills of an authentic leader's repertoire.

YOUR NEW HEALTH REGIMEN

Earn respect by building trust and showing people you value them.

Build trust by making decisions and acting in a way that shows integrity, honesty, fairness, and consistency.

Be approachable and maintain your humility.

Be committed to connecting with and developing people as the single most important thing you do in your leadership role.

Do the hard work of creating a people development culture and watch your team's performance and bottom-line results improve.

Respect others, and they will respect you; remember that it is a two-way street.

Find a way to obtain constructive criticism and be seen to act on the feedback.

PRESCRIPTION 2

THE CURE FOR EMPLOYEES
WITH BAD ATTITUDES

IN THE BUSINESS world, "bad attitude" is a catchall category for a lot of tough people problems: unwillingness to work with others, lack of initiative, fear of failure that leads to lack of confidence, low morale, or a general lack of motivation that can result from a variety of circumstances. Sometimes the problem behind a bad attitude resides solely with the infected employee, but often the problem is much larger and requires a holistic approach to improve the mood within the team or organization.

Tackling problems of attitude is a tough challenge for leaders because there are so many potential contributors to the problem. But if you have a problem with attitude, motivation, or morale in your team, your first step had better be to put into practice what you learned in Prescription 1, because earning employees' respect by respecting them goes a long way toward ensuring positive attitudes and high levels of motivation and morale.

Lab Work

A new survey by Sirota Survey Intelligence, along with the authors of *The Enthusiastic Employee*, David Sirota, Louis A. Mischkind, and Michael Irwin Meltzer, indicates respect goes a long way when it comes to morale (Durett, 2006).

The results of the survey of 370,378 employees showed that 63 percent of employees who feel their employers do not treat them with respect think about and/or plan to leave their positions within a two-year time frame; only 19 percent who feel their employers treat them like adults intend to leave.

Respect also translates into employee enthusiasm. Employees who reported that they feel "very good" about how they are treated at work are more than three times as enthusiastic as those who feel just "good" about it.

If you're working on Prescription 1 already and still have attitude problems in your team, the second prescription I can offer is:

R︎X If you want to improve the attitudes of the people on your team, you need to identify and correct potential negative contributors in the organization, make sure you offer fair compensation, model the attitude and behaviors you want your team to emulate, build a culture that supports positive attitudes and work habits, and consistently work to improve motivation and morale.

IDENTIFY THE PROBLEM

While it's possible that an attitude problem exists only with one or two employees, it's often the case that there is a larger systemic problem that's contributing to low motivation or morale within a team or organization. Probably the biggest contributor to stress and anxiety within an organization is change, and we all know that in this fast-paced world, change is inevitable and becoming more rapid.

Every business goes through phases in the development cycle, and in each one there is the potential to energize or demotivate employees. The way a team reacts to each situation has a lot to do with how that particular phase is viewed and handled by the leader. For example, a rapid-growth phase might present the following challenges:

- Stress and anxiety with coworkers
- New employees needing mentoring and training
- Strain to meet customer demands
- Loss of service quality
- Product delays
- Longer working hours

It is not unusual for a business experiencing a period of change, such as a rapid-growth phase, to find employees becoming frustrated. If the leader is not right on top of this situation, the frustration may turn to anger and demotivation, particularly if the period of change is a long one.

Employees want to know that their leader has a sense of how to get them through tough times. Good leaders are confident, imaginative, inspirational, and courageous in challenging times, and they have the ability to turn negative energy into positive energy.

If your team or organization is working through a period of major change, you will need to think very hard about how to build morale and motivation throughout the change. Talk to your employees to find out what their concerns are. Share as much information with them as you possibly can. Be open and available. If there are specific concerns that seem to resonate with many of your team members, do what you can to alleviate those concerns. But most importantly, you must work to model the positive attitude and behaviors you want your team to emulate. While this is particularly important during times of change, it is always a key element of authentic leadership and maintaining morale and motivation.

OFFER FAIR COMPENSATION

Countless research projects over many years, the activities of labor unions, and common sense tell us that your people will not be motivated or have high morale if their remuneration is significantly below industry standards. In fact, on my list of why people stay with a company (the complete list is offered in the next section) fair compensation is pretty high up.

You need to continually research similar companies within your industry and get up-to-date details on their total remuneration packages—salaries, bonus structures, and benefits. If your compensation model is not competitive, change it.

I don't believe that to retain your people you have to offer the best pay in your industry. But if your people know that their pay is unfair compared to industry standards, they will be discontented.

Lab Work

The one hundred top employers listed annually in *Fortune* magazine set themselves apart by the benefits and incentives they offer their employees. For example, Google was listed as the number-one company in 2007. Google offers free meals, a swimming pool and spa, and free doctors' visits on-site; also, engineers can spend 20 percent of their time on independent projects. The number-two company, Genetech, offers six-week paid sabbaticals to employees every six years. At the Container Store (third), "family friendly" shifts are offered, from 9 a.m. to 2 p.m., allowing for school drop-offs and pick-ups; nearly a tenth of all employees take advantage of it. W. L. Gore & Associates (tenth) focuses on promoting from within; CEO Terri L. Kelly joined Gore as a process engineer in 1983 ("100 Best Companies to Work for 2007," *Fortune*, 2007).

Your most talented team members will be subject to continual headhunting from your competitors, or they'll put feelers out themselves for something with better pay.

Though employees should always be paid competitively, keep in mind that you need to do more than offer fair and competitive salaries. The law firm where my daughter is a lawyer is an example of a business that focuses too much on competitive remuneration.

This firm targeted the best law students, and it was considered a compliment to be offered a position with them. Three years later, of more than thirty new recruits from her induction class, there are only three left, despite the firm's top salaries. There are obviously reasons other than money that explain why they are not retaining their people.

Don't believe that you can use great salaries to make up for the lack of a motivating, rewarding, respectful work environment. And don't think that you can use reward or recognition programs to make up for low salaries (see next section). Uncompetitive remuneration makes your reward and recognition programs seem trivial, and people will be cynical about rewards if they feel that they're being used as a way to buy their loyalty when they know their compensation is off the pace.

SET THE TONE

Of course, money is only part of the picture of an employee's attitude. The most important thing you can do as a leader is set the tone and mood within your team. It all starts with your mood. As a leader, how you feel and what you do will flow and vibrate through your whole working environment. You may not be able to fix every bad attitude, but on a daily basis, whether you realize it or not, you are putting out vibes that will influence every employee's attitude, either positively or negatively. If you take every opportunity to show good attitude and behaviors at work, your team will follow that example—and feel good about it.

With new employees, it is crucial that a leader immediately establish a motivational tone through her mood, passion, and personal enthusiasm. This positive attitude will have an uplifting effect on your new people, giving them confidence that they selected the right company.

Leaders create a positive environment and exhibit a positive attitude through communication, empathy, and an intimate awareness of their team's perception of their work.

Communication

The words a leader uses have a profound effect on individual and team attitude by clearly reflecting the leader's attitude and what he expects of others. Following are some guidelines to keep in mind when communicating with your team:

- Whenever appropriate, phrase your communication in terms of the needs of and benefits for the team; use *we*, not *I*.
- Show your team members that you appreciate the work they do; say "thank you" often.
- Praise team members, specifically, whenever possible.
- Show that you are open to feedback by asking for team members' opinions.
- When a team member does an excellent job, let the entire team know. One of these public praise moments can result in days of increased productivity because the singled-out employee feels valued and special.

Empathy

You won't be able to be empathetic if you don't really know and understand each of your team members as an individual. Remember the key point from Prescription 1: you have to honestly and authentically connect with each of your employees whenever possible.

Showing empathy isn't about letting go of your needs. It simply means you are able to see things from the other person's perspective and acknowledge their feelings. William Ury, in his book *Getting Past No,* makes the point that it is important to see both the factual reality and the feelings of another person. He uses this illustration:

> Employee says, "I just found out Dale makes two thousand dollars more than I do for the same job." But trying to explain why Dale makes more money, even if there are valid reasons, will only make the employee angrier. Instead, you must acknowledge the fact and the feelings first: "You think we are taking advantage of you and you're angry. I can understand that. I'd probably feel the same way." An angry person doesn't expect that response. By acknowledging their feelings you've calmed them down. His next statement might be "Well, I don't earn as much as Dale," which shows he's ready to hear your explanation.

Being empathetic toward your team members will help them be more empathetic toward each other and you, which will improve the cohesiveness of your team and improve the tone of the environment.

Perception

If you think about it, all of the ingredients needed for a great business boil down to a few basic requirements: good people selection and development; excellent strategy, mission, vision, and values; great products, service, and marketing; and you and your employees feeling great about your work.

You can have all the other key business drivers in place, but for the business to perform exceptionally, your people have to *feel* inspired, excited, enthusiastic, and creative, as well as that they are contributing to the success of the business.

How people perceive their organization is directly affected by their leaders' mood. How the leaders feel affects how the workers feel and determines the overall tone of the culture.

So the first step in respecting and affecting your team members' feelings about their work is being open to your own feelings and seeking ways to make sure those feelings are positive. You have to move from your head (analysis, reaction, emotion) to your heart (true feelings). Following are some ways to do that:

- Do fun things; laugh.

- Recognize others; it will make you feel good.

- Be gentle with yourself; don't be too hard on yourself when one of your decisions doesn't turn out the way you expected.

- Keep learning; the more you know the more confident you'll feel in your decisions.

- Balance your life; if you don't, you won't be able to control your stress levels.

- Make others feel great by truly connecting with them through actions such as
    - Listening to what they say with an eye toward how they are feeling;
    - Smiling as much as possible;
    - Being present, available, and open;
    - Acknowledging, acknowledging, acknowledging;
    - Making them feel safe;
    - Controlling your emotions; and
    - Being humble.

People will forget what you say. They will forget what you
do. But they will never forget how you made them feel.
—CARL W. BUECHNER, AUTHOR AND CLERGYMAN

ONCE YOU'VE ANALYZED your own attitude and behaviors and feel confident that you are setting a positive tone that will spread throughout your team, the next step is to build a positive culture and environment that supports the types of attitudes and behaviors you want your team members to exhibit.

BUILD A CULTURE OF COLLABORATION AND INITIATIVE

Inspiring collaboration and initiative in your team is a surefire way to improve attitudes. When people feel that they can rely on their teammates and that their involvement and initiative are expected and will be rewarded, their attitudes toward the work they do will skyrocket, even in challenging times.

Collaboration is particularly crucial to today's business environment. As globalization and competition intensify, business becomes more about relationships and networks, making internal and external collaboration essential. There will be more time spent applying critical thinking and really understanding the effects of collaboration, as in this new world people will need to develop personal leadership skills to help improve the performance of increasingly scattered work groups and to maximize the effectiveness of outsourcing as globalization and decentralization take hold. Without an effective collaboration plan, one hand will not know what the other is doing. Currently we see this when dealing with companies that have outsourced overseas: customers have to deal with language issues and the frustration of repeating their concern to many different people and departments. Successful businesses of the future will overcome these issues by linking all areas of the business together to ensure a collaborated approach.

But collaboration does not come easily in many organizations. For projects to have the best chance of success, a leader has to ensure that all players, internal and external, are working together. The leader's role is to ensure that the culture facilitates collaborating and cooperating to deliver the desired outcomes. She needs to be the role model for openness, information sharing, clear communication to all levels, and displaying trust and integrity. The astute leader will ensure that excellent relationships are created internally and externally to build a dynamic network in which all parties thrive.

Many leaders hoping to foster collaboration invest in integrated communication technologies to help their teams share information. However, while technology will help your people collaborate efficiently with their coworkers on business processes and projects, it is not the key to effective collaboration. The key is the example of the business leaders.

Business leaders need to demonstrate that their commitment to collaboration is strong, yet ensure that they do not stifle individual contributions. Initiatives and ideas need to be encouraged from individuals on all levels of the company. A culture of initiative is a culture of continuous improvement. This means leaders are continually working on developing people, instilling confidence and displaying trust, and encouraging even less-senior employees to use their initiative, thereby accessing the combined brainpower of the entire team. When all employees are focusing their abilities and imaginations on the problem at hand, it will have a marked effect on performance. If a company is facing concerns, one of the most powerful steps you can take is to focus *all* your team on providing solutions. Harnessing the brainpower of the entire team through proactive meetings dedicated to providing ideas, initiatives, and solutions to the issues rather than focusing on the problems has a profound effect.

 Pick up your pace 25 percent, lift up your head, put a smile on your *face, and remember you are either on the way or in the way.*
—KEITH "DR. ATTITUDE" HARRELL, AUTHOR
AND MOTIVATIONAL SPEAKER

One of a leader's key attributes is the ability to influence others, and successful leaders use this skill to encourage employees to take the initiative in decision making. This is not to take accountability away from the leader. It is more a way to encourage employees to think things through and bring recommendations to their supervisor when the decision is outside the employee's scope of control. Following is an example of an employee taking initiative.

An employee goes to his supervisor and says, "I'd like your input on a situation. To give you an overview, we had an unusual request from a valued client yesterday to provide a service that we do not normally provide. On the surface it looked feasible, but I put together a list of questions to be considered before we commit. Based on the answers to these questions I have narrowed it down to three options. We can approve the request, decline the request, or work with them to provide a win-win outcome. Can you and I schedule some time together this afternoon or tomorrow morning so I can get back to the client by the end of the business day tomorrow?"

This example displays a high level of initiative and the positive outcomes a culture of initiative can offer, such as enhancing employee confidence, attitude, and job satisfaction; creating speedier results through an efficient use of management's time; and providing an opportunity for the organization to determine other possible solutions and services that create win-win outcomes for clients and the business.

Some employees will be ready to take the initiative like this right away, while others will need training, coaching, and encouragement to reach this level. Give more autonomy as employees earn it by developing creative approaches to issues, setting challenging objectives, and exceeding standards, and they will love coming to work.

As your people gain confidence in this new culture, they will feel their jobs being enriched. In turn this job enrichment will encourage more initiative, changing what they do and how they do it. As they continue to grow, it will be critical to involve them in the decision-making process of planning and setting budgets. This gives employees room to be creative and set their own challenging goals, encourages further self-development, and allows them to see themselves as an integral part of the big picture, which builds trust and loyalty.

An initiative culture will encourage participation, so be prepared for issues like the following to be raised:

- Request for an employee consultative committee
- Input in decisions before they are finalized
- Contact with clients to hear their perspectives

- Demands for greater autonomy
- Participation in setting of team goals
- Career planning
- Flexible working hours
- Employee incentives

A leader has to be careful how these requests for participation are handled; it is very important that this is done respectfully to protect the developing initiative culture and to ensure that the rising people power is not halted. Don't be afraid to include employees in the planning process and setting budgets.

I have used an "Employee Suggestion Initiative" often with outstanding success. This can be done through a "suggestion box," or brainstorming sessions at team meetings when you want to focus on a particular issue. These processes give frontline employees the opportunity to participate in making decisions. You can use this kind of initiative generally or on specific issues, but it is very important that you provide public recognition to people who provide workable suggestions. The recognition is essential, and if the culture has not been one of sharing ideas before now, you may need to kick this program off with monetary rewards as well. In the past I have received invaluable suggestions enabling us to improve workplace efficiency, customer service, and products, to reduce expenditures, and to enhance revenue.

ONCE YOU'VE CHECKED your own attitude and have begun work on the culture in your team or organization, you can address specific issues of motivation and morale for individual team members and the team as a whole.

IMPROVE MOTIVATION

The word *motivation* literally means "a reason to move," and pretty much every move we make has a reason behind it: we sleep when we are tired, we eat when hungry, and we drink when thirsty. Leaders who want to motivate their people don't have to be trained psychologists, but they do need an excellent understanding of human behavior. It's a fact that people are motivated by different needs, and a leader who is connected, in touch, with his team members will understand their individual motivators. The leader who truly has a heart connection with his team will know more than their motivators; he will know their dreams. When we get to the level of helping our people achieve their dreams, motivation and morale will be excellent.

The biggest mistake managers make in trying to motivate their teams is to assume that money is their people's key motivator. To be a good leader, you must find your people's hot buttons—their individual reasons for striving to achieve—by asking questions and listening attentively to the answers.

> All things being equal, you can attract, retain, and motivate the best and brightest by recognizing that what motivates me might not motivate you.
>
> —JOHN PUTZIER, AUTHOR OF *GET WEIRD!*

That said, most people are motivated to some degree by one or more of the following nine needs:

- **Achievement and growth:** People motivated by this need want to use their talents for success. They desire to grow through learning new roles or educating themselves. Provide challenging projects suited to their skills and they will constantly achieve.

- **Money:** People motivated by money desire to earn substantial income. Give these people remuneration systems that reward achievement, bonuses that reward exceeding expectations, or an open-ended commission structure based on performance.

- **Teamwork:** People motivated by this need enjoy being part of a successful team. They enjoy interacting with people; group projects motivate them, as does the social aspect of the workplace.

- **Power or ego:** People motivated by this need enjoy controlling and influencing others. They thrive on making decisions and being in a position to lead and direct others. Beware enabling this desire too early, however, as wanting power does not necessarily make someone a good leader.

- **Approval:** People motivated by the need for approval need recognition and praise. Give them positive feedback and public recognition of their achievements and contributions. Ensure that this feedback is genuine and heartfelt as employees can easily detect insincere approval or recognition, and this will be a demotivator.

- **Security:** People motivated by security want a steady income, solid benefits, and a stable workplace. Give these people attractive base salaries and a comfortable work environment with low risk. Do not place these people in positions where income is primarily performance based or in commission-only roles.

- **Independence:** People motivated by this need want autonomy and freedom to choose their own work hours and love to work alone. These people will enjoy roles like being a mobile team member and may desire opportunities for them to work from home.

- **Stability:** People motivated by a desire for stability want to work in a position where there is minimal disruption and change. Do not place them in roles where change is rapid or day-to-day duties are radically different. Their ideal is a stable role with set schedules and minimum disruption.

- **Equality:** People motivated by this need desire fair treatment. They will analyze and compare their duties, work hours, salary, and benefits to those of other employees and may become disenchanted if they regard themselves as disadvantaged.

In addition to these nine basic drivers, there is another element of the new workplace that can be a big motivator for some people. In the modern business world, flexibility is paramount to organizational success. Create and encourage flexibility in the workplace—flexible hours, flexible work location (working from home), flexible arrangements for certain duties, etc. Many employees will not approach employers for fear of being perceived as not committed to their jobs, but this flexibility may be something that they desperately want or need. A Families and Work Institute study indicated that 39 percent of the U.S. workforce believed that taking advantage of flexibility programs would result in less pay and fewer opportunities to be promoted (McNulty, 2006). If your employees feel that you promote and support flexible work situations, they'll be more likely to stay on and be motivated when they experience major life changes, such as having children, moving to a new home, having to take care of an elderly parent, etc.

If you are concerned about the attitude or motivation level of a particular employee, take some time to honestly assess what you think motivates this person. If you aren't sure, analyze his work habits, identify his strengths (which are often related to key motivators), and have a conversation with him. When you have analyzed your employee's motivating hot buttons or learned his dreams, it is time to become innovative. You need to structure his role and rewards to match his needs.

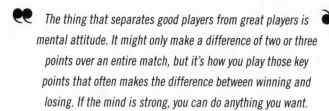

The thing that separates good players from great players is mental attitude. It might only make a difference of two or three points over an entire match, but it's how you play those key points that often makes the difference between winning and losing. If the mind is strong, you can do anything you want.

—CHRIS EVERT, CHAMPION TENNIS PLAYER

While this is an important tool to use in solving attitude or motivation problems with individuals, it's also something that should be taken into account for every employee, particularly new hires. If you spend the time early on in an employee's career to ensure that her role, her compensation, and the structure of her position are in line with her key motivators, you'll be well on your way to a team member who is motivated, happy, and positive.

How to Motivate Different Generations

One of the biggest challenges facing today's leaders is that for the first time, they could be managing four distinct generations with

🧪 Lab Work

According to Gallup Organization research, only 20 percent of employees in large organizations surveyed felt their strengths were utilized on a daily basis; eight out of ten felt like square pegs placed in round holes.

Do you know how much revenue a company loses when employees are unmotivated and unengaged? According to the Gallup Organization, disengaged workers cost American business an estimated $292 billion to $355 billion a year! They also report that only 25 percent of employees are engaged at work (Russel, 2005); that leaves 75 percent of employees disconnected in the workplace every day.

According to *The Enthusiastic Employee*, a book that reports on thirty years of employee surveys, the three principal goals of workers are to experience equity and fair treatment; to feel pride and achievement in one's job and help the company to succeed; and to feel a sense of camaraderie in the working environment ("Worker Myths Companies Accept," *Training & Development*, 2005).

four distinct common motivators. Matures, Baby Boomers, Gen Xers, and Gen Yers are all in the workforce right now. These groups have different values and provide different challenges for leaders in getting to know their traits and manage them effectively.

Of course, you should not generalize and manage your people according to the stereotypes of their particular group. But smart organizations and leaders obtain information on the values of these different generations to use as a starting point. This knowledge will be a great base to start from, but all leaders must take into account employee individuality and not generalize how they treat people in a specific generation. We need to be careful not to stereotype workers, but leaders need to understand what may be motivating factors for people of different age groups.

Organizations must also build relationships and manage based on a basic understanding of the traits of age-based cohorts to be successful in the current business atmosphere. Tailoring broad-reaching management tactics according to cohort characteristics can be beneficial (McNulty, 2006).

Following are some key characteristics from a variety of studies of various age groups:

- Workers under thirty-five are less loyal to institutions and want responsibility and the chance to offer input right away. They are not afraid to make decisions, and their relationship with their immediate manager supersedes the one with the organization. Place employees from this group in positions of responsibility right away. Anticipate that this group will leave to pursue education, other employment opportunities, travel, etc.; make it easy for them to return.

- Workers between thirty-five and fifty-four are antiauthoritarian, idealistic, ambitious, flexible, industrious, independent, and people centered. This group distrusts leadership, spends a lot of time negotiating busy lives, and wants merit-based pay systems and participative management. This group usually comprises middle managers who will stay in their roles longer because the older generations are working longer. Provide new opportunities, mentoring roles, and knowledge sharing. Consider compensating them for transferring to lateral positions as a retention program.

- Workers over fifty-five trust authority, respect rules, are loyal to institutions, expect people to "pay their dues" before receiving authority, value financial security, have difficulty with ambiguity, and have strong social skills. This group should be interacting with people and utilizing its expertise and historical perspective. Offer members of this group the chance to master new skills, and be sensitive to younger professionals managing older workers.

Motivating Teams

Now that we have a plan to motivate individuals, let's look at motivating teams. While team motivation begins and ends with motivating individuals, the team will be highly motivated and most effective when the following apply:

- Each person is a willing member of the team.
- Each person sees being a team member as personally rewarding.
- The team is challenged to produce its best.
- Team meetings are productive, with honest input from all members.
- Each team member takes pride in being part of the team.
- Each team member has a sense of group accountability.
- Each team member takes pride in the team achieving its intentions.
- The team celebrates its successes together.

An excellent leader will reflect the success of the team back to the team. Remember, one of the prime character traits of a great leader is humility.

Motivation in Special Cases

Every leader has had an employee situation that appeared hopeless. Motivating some individuals can seem like a daunting task. But few cases are beyond rehabilitation. Let's look at a couple of examples.

CASE STUDY: Mary

Mary, a trusted administrator with ten years of service, is finding it increasingly difficult to juggle her home life and work commitments due to a recent change in residence that increases her round-trip commute to almost two hours. You see the writing on the wall that Mary is likely to leave, but she is a valuable member of your team and you would hate to see her go. There are a few steps you can take to motivate Mary to stay. Approach Mary about flexible work hours that will enable her to avoid peak traffic and reduce commute times by half. Consider setting up a home office and change Mary's work to incorporate duties that can be completed off-site, even if only part-time.

CASE STUDY: Bill

Bill is a long-standing, respected employee who is very popular within the team. He has eighteen months until retirement and knows that he has reached the ceiling regarding promotion and income levels. Achievement in his current role is not a motivator because he feels he has achieved plenty and appears to be coasting to retirement. You cannot dismiss Bill due to nonperformance, as he is doing just enough to retain his position.

And due to his popularity, if you tried to force him out on performance issues, others would see this as getting rid of someone who has given loyal service for many years.

Meet with Bill over coffee and let him know how you feel about his loyal service. Tell him you would like to work with him to design a role that would take advantage of his immense experience and skills across a wide range of roles in the organization. A win-win situation could be one of the following:

- Time-bound special projects that will show a short-term result. It is important that Bill sees that his efforts are clearly measurable and that results will occur before he leaves.

- Put him in a mentoring role so he can teach new employees. It is critical to let him know the importance of this role in helping new people start with passion and a positive attitude as he passes on his invaluable experience. Structure rewards for him based on the success of the new employees.

While trying to motivate people who seem unmotivated is a special challenge, another special challenge is maintaining focus on motivating people who seem not to need it. High achievers have an inner drive; they are self-motivated because they know what they want and sometimes, by chance, they are in a role that matches their motivating factors. Their success usually comes from executing the basics superbly, day in and day out. They are consistent high achievers, but that doesn't mean you shouldn't seek out ways to continually motivate them. Try utilizing them as role models in training sessions at your skills workshops. Most high achievers are delighted to do this, since it plays to their ego and also will help them hone their skills even more as they prepare and deliver presentations. An important part of a coach's job is to help stars shine while keeping their egos under control. A good way of doing this is by offering no special concessions and not being afraid to have "courageous conversations" with employees displaying excessive ego if they step out of line. High achievers will also have dreams beyond their current success. If you can help them achieve their dreams, it is an excellent way to truly connect with them—and to aid retention of these top performers.

MOTIVATING PEOPLE DOES take ongoing work, but put your people in the right enriched roles and your efforts will be repaid with a more dedicated and loyal workforce, lower turnover, and higher productivity.

 People say motivation doesn't last. Well neither does bathing—that's why we recommend it daily.
—ZIG ZIGLAR, MOTIVATIONAL SPEAKER

IMPROVE MORALE

We all know that working in a place where morale is high makes us feel great. Results are superior in a positive atmosphere. However, workplace morale will be decimated if the leader does not set a positive example and keep his or her emotions in check. Exhibit passion, enthusiasm, and a positive spirit (combined with a liberal dose of humility, sincere recognition, and proof you are operating from the heart), and you will see a team with high morale. Keep in mind that as you develop your people and improve results, morale will climb. Everyone loves to be part of a winning team or a successful company.

You will know morale is low when your team members think, speak, and act in terms of *I don't*, such as "I don't feel appreciated," "I don't get the support I need," or "I don't think anybody would care if I left." If any of your team members are feeling this way, it is only a matter of time before they leave.

One of the best pieces of practical leadership advice comes from Ken Blanchard and Spencer Johnson's *The One-Minute Manager:* "Catch someone doing something right and tell them about it." I love this quote, because recognition is an excellent driver. There are too many managers focused on catching somebody doing something wrong and telling them about it.

 Choose a job you love, and you'll never have to work a day in your life.
—CONFUCIUS

Overcoming Negativity

To combat negativity, there are certain types of thinking you need to train out of yourself and your team. Remember, you set the tone, so start with your own morale first.

- **Ignoring the small positives:** Don't filter out good indications and turn these signs and signals into negatives. Even if it is only a small win, celebrate it and focus your team on the positive.

- **All-or-nothing thinking:** Don't categorize events, behaviors, or characteristics in black-and-white terminology: good/bad, success/failure, winners/losers. There are lots of shades of gray in the world, and all-or-nothing thinking can rule out all the opportunities that exist in the gray areas.

- **Mind reading:** Do not assume that you know other people's points of view. Simply ask them. You'll often be surprised by how much more negative your assumptions were than the reality.

- **Rigid thinking:** Don't be dogged or stuck in an idea, feeling, or belief without looking at alternatives; it will lead to negativity in the long term because you'll miss out on key opportunities.

- **Catastrophic thinking:** Don't assume the worst will happen or rehearse this undesirable outcome in your head. We attract the outcomes we focus on, so focus on the positive, like top sports players who rehearse the perfect execution in their minds to achieve their intended outcome.

In my opinion a positive attitude is the single most important attribute a person can have. With a positive attitude, anything is possible. Learning becomes enjoyable and easier, and the workplace has a joyful atmosphere when there is a positive spirit. Let's look at some behaviors to encourage if negativity surfaces.

- **Planning:** A clear plan and structured milestones to show achievement along the way promote confidence.

- **Let negative people be lonely:** Refuse to associate with negative people. If you have a negative person on your team, do everything you can to rehabilitate that person. If you cannot turn her around and in your heart you know that you have tried everything possible, then it is time to dismiss the "bad apple" before her attitude affects the entire team.

- **Positive self-talk:** Congratulate yourself and your team along the journey to a goal; highlight the positives and coach yourself and your team to achieve your potential.

- **Take action:** All it takes is one step to begin moving out of the paralysis that negativity induces. Take bold action and encourage your team to do likewise.

- **If you say so:** Every time you frame one of your skills or attributes in a bad light, say to yourself, "If you say so." (For instance, "I am unlucky, I am a failure, I'll never understand this—If you say so!") It is amazing how this changes your thinking. When one of your team members is berating himself, use the same tactic. You'll be amazed at how quickly he'll realize what he's doing to himself. Just be sure he doesn't think you are being serious or snide. Follow it up by explaining that you have every confidence in his ability.

You don't want to encourage pessimism, but be sure not to alienate people by not listening to their concerns. Be sure you are not dismissing an employee's legitimate concerns as a negative attitude. For example, don't sweep operational problems under the "negative attitude" rug. Instead, listen to dissenters to determine if issues are true problems that you must solve on your level. If they are not, then drill down to the real issues so they can be diffused. Similarly, whistle-blowing should be investigated immediately so problems and issues can be dealt with appropriately. Listen to your employees' problems and show support, empathy, compassion, and care.

 The difference between a positive spirit and a positive attitude is *that one comes from the heart and the other from the head.*
—AMANDA GORE, MOTIVATIONAL SPEAKER AND CONNECTION EXPERT

Building Confidence

Another important component of your role as a leader is the ability to lift the confidence of your people and remove fear of failure. Fear can lead to mind-numbing paralysis among some very capable people. The best way to remove fear is by showing, without a doubt and at every opportunity, that you believe in your people and their capacities to develop. This requires you to emphasize the following truths:

- Everyone fails at times.
- Failure can lead to growth and improvement.
- Success requires risk.
- Simple mistakes do not constitute failure.
- It's essential to learn from mistakes and move on.

To become an authentic leader, you will need to focus—without fail—on building confidence and self-esteem. You can become a source of inspiration for your people only by demonstrating constant support for and participation in their working lives.

I remember a time when a leader reporting to me made a mistake that would potentially cost our company two hundred thousand dollars. At the meeting with me he expected to be fired. I asked what he had learned from this experience, and he listed a number of things that he would do differently next time. These recommendations were well thought out and showed the experience had been valuable to him. He waited for my reaction, and then asked if I was going to terminate him. I asked him, "Why would I fire a valuable employee when we have just invested a huge amount in his learning?"

Tips for Lifting Morale

A key component of morale is rewarding and recognizing employees, and we'll discuss that in detail when covering ways to prevent employees from abandoning ship. Following are some great tips for improving morale in almost any situation:

- To combat negativity, brainstorm with your team on all of the possible positive outcomes or opportunities that might result from the situation.

- To combat fear of failure, share any of your failures with your team and ask for suggestions on how to solve the problem or how you should have handled the situation differently. You may learn something important, and your team won't be afraid to share their failures with you.

- Create an achievements box and have everyone fill it with slips describing significant wins: customer service stories, great sales results, projects completed, personal accomplishments, etc. Read these out at weekly team meetings, and to encourage participation, have random drawings for movie tickets, chocolates, or bottles of wine. People forget the positives if you fail to relive them.

- Truly connect with your people by discovering their dreams and helping them achieve them.

- Create a board where people can post emails or other correspondence with praise from internal or external clients. Make sure employees share the correspondence with you so you can post it if they don't.

- Look for ways to create a fun atmosphere in the office: morning teas or coffee breaks to celebrate success; divide into teams and have lunchtime or end-of-day games like a golf-putting competition or throwing tennis balls into a rubbish bin; have theater nights or bowling nights; have meetings outside the office; rotate 25 percent of staff to start an hour later on Mondays. Be innovative and think of fun activities that everyone can be involved in.

 Daring ideas are like chessmen moved forward: they may be beaten, but they may start a winning game.
—JOHANN WOLFGANG VON GOETHE

MY HOPE IS that you understand the importance of leaders as positive role models. Whether it is the moods they display, their attitudes, their passion, or their ability to focus on the positive, they are constantly under the spotlight and their teams will respond in ways that reflect their own demeanor. If you are battling issues of attitude, motivation, and morale, consider the tone you are setting, the culture you've built, and what you are doing every day to motivate your team and build morale.

YOUR NEW HEALTH REGIMEN

Model the attitude and behaviors you want your people to exhibit.

Analyze your own mood and the effect it has on your team.

Maintain your humility as a leader; spread recognition to your team.

Inspire people with your passion, enthusiasm, and excitement.

Be authentic and honest in your communication.

Identify organizational problems that might be affecting attitudes or behaviors; help employees through ambiguous and stressful times of change.

Build a culture of collaboration and initiative to support the types of attitudes and behaviors you want to promote.

Discover what motivates your employees; you may initially hear "more money," but continue to peel away the onion to find out what else inspires them. Money is rarely the whole answer.

Innovatively build key motivators into each individual's position.

Create the appropriate stimulus for team motivation.

Never let pessimism influence your positive approach or your employees' motivation.

PRESCRIPTION 3

THE CURE FOR
DISCONTENTED EMPLOYEES

 HAVING DISCONTENTED EMPLOYEES is one of the worst problems a leader can face because it can result in high turnover, which is incredibly costly. In fact, losing quality employees affects the bottom line more significantly than any other human resource issue. At the Families and Work Institute, a nonprofit research organization that addresses the changing nature of work and family life, experts tell company leaders that it will cost about 75 percent of a nonmanagerial worker's annual salary to replace her and 150 percent of a manager's annual salary.

You may be thinking, "You've already talked about employees who lack respect and have poor attitudes. Isn't a discontented employee the same thing?" No, definitely not. You can have an employee who respects your leadership, has a great attitude, and is highly motivated, but still isn't content—and that can lead to the loss of one of your best employees. Contentment as an employee means that you are happy where you are. An employee's discontentment with a position can certainly lead to problems with attitude

🧪 Lab Work

In the United States, 83 percent of companies are concerned about recruiting and retaining talented employees. The largest companies (seven thousand or more employees) are especially troubled, with 95.5 percent saying this issue is important to them. The health-care industry (94.5 percent) and educational firms (92.3 percent) are also struggling in this area ("How to Get and Keep the Best Employees," *HR Focus*, 2006).

and respect if nothing is done to solve the problem, but it's really a more subtle issue than the first two ailments we've discussed, and it will hit you hard in the bottom line.

In terms of recruitment and retention, in addition to the hard costs of turnover, there are soft costs that are harder to track, although they are just as real and have a strong impact on an organization. Poor recruitment or retention can lead to weakened customer relationships, lost opportunity costs, lowered team morale, loss of momentum, potential loss of other employees, and lost production. The actual dollar cost is debatable, but there is no debate that turnover is a huge cost to business.

That's why the third prescription I'm offering is:

R͓x If you want to have happy, content employees who stay for the long term, you need to hire well, use creative and proactive methods to retain your most valued team members, and use recognition and reward programs to let employees know how much they are valued.

HIRE SMART

Hiring the best person for a position—doing everything you can to ensure that your new hire is a good fit for the position in terms of experience, skills, attitude, personality, and key motivators—is the first critical step to having contented employees and reducing turnover. Selecting the right people is an absolutely critical part to the success of any business. If you have the right people in the right positions, everything else in the business will flow relatively smoothly. Conversely, if you hire the wrong people or place good people in the wrong positions, no matter how great your products and ideas are, the business will not achieve its optimum potential, and turnover costs will be a drain on the success you do achieve.

If you think about the potential costs in time and lost production when we hire the wrong person, you'll understand that making the right selection is critical. Think of all the costs of hiring:

- Staff preparing and executing the hiring process
- Advertising
- Fielding calls and doing initial screening
- Creating and staffing recruitment showcases
- Three rounds of interviews, with more interviewers involved at each level
- Reference checking
- Background checking
- Induction training
- Ongoing training to learn the role
- Specialized training sessions
- Mentor downtime while coaching a new hire
- Lower productivity while a new hire is in training

Then, of course, there are the following costs of making a wrong selection:

- If the poor hire is a manager or leader, the cost to morale and motivation of their team
- Performance management—your time and the time of other specialists
- Your time, HR's time, and your lawyer's time spent developing a strategy to remove the poor hire from the role
- Cost of separation package to release the employee
- Salary paid for employee's poor performance
- Loss of production due to poor performance and upheaval
- Remotivating staff directly affected by the issue
- Rebuilding workforce morale
- RESTARTING THE PROCESS!

Having the right process and ensuring that all people involved in recruitment and selection stick rigidly to it can potentially save your business hundreds of thousands of dollars. So let's take a look at the basics for a sound recruitment and selection process.

Create a Basic Recruitment and Selection Process

The following is a basic recruitment and selection process. Obviously, for high-level or specialized roles, this process should be expanded to fit the role's level of responsibility and impact on the organization. Spending a few extra hours on the selection process is well worth it; if you disagree, just consider the months you might spend on performance management to rehabilitate or release a poor selection.

❶ Workforce Numbers

The starting point in any recruitment process should be determining your optimum workforce numbers—the number that will

- grow the business effectively (don't throw people at a problem if the difficulty is with your operational process);
- allow your people to be productive, earn a good income, and have great self-esteem; and
- offer the best span of control (the number of people reporting to each manager) for your particular business.

Don't hire more people than you need. If you do, you might be faced with a future downsizing that affects morale. Grow smart!

❷ Skills/Attributes

Develop a skills/attributes list for each role by interviewing and benchmarking your high and low performers. If you are replacing an employee, take a look at that person's exit interview notes to see if it holds any insight into the position that you may be missing. When compiling the list of skills and attributes, also obtain feedback from the customers and supervisors of the person or people in this role whenever possible. This will make the list well rounded. And don't forget to include soft attributes like good attitude and personality. This list should comprise positive aspects that you will look for and negative aspects that will knock a person out of contention. Do not lower your standards!

Build your own job description or work with human resources to create one from your list of attributes. A detailed internal position description helps match candidate skills during interviews.

❸ Locate Talent

Depending on the size of your business and the number of people you want to recruit, the best way to locate talent may be through a search firm, an employment agency, an online job bank, or advertisements in local and regional newspapers and other media. Regardless of your approach, you should always use the following three methods in your search:

- Have an incentive system in place to encourage members of your current workforce to refer people. Link rewards to the success of the recruit. Your people know what it takes to be successful in their roles and will only refer people who they are convinced will be successful. Following up on these referrals is critical, however, as it is embarrassing to your current employee if you do not make prompt contact with this potential recruit.

- Use your centers of influence to obtain referrals for prospective recruits—for example, from your customers or suppliers.

- Ensure that you and your team members keep your eyes open as you go about your daily lives. Look for that person who has something special and would fit into a role within your business.

Keep digging until you have a healthy number of résumés from which to select. Extra effort on the front end will save headaches on the back end of the hiring process.

❹ Initial Screening

Develop a basic set of guidelines for the screening process to pare down the possible candidates. Ensure that the people doing the initial screening are matching the skills in the position description with the experience and attributes of the candidate when deciding to retain or remove applicants at this initial stage. Screening rules should be applied equitably. For example, does the description allow years of experience to be exchangeable with years of education, or can certain volunteer experiences be counted toward work experience?

❺ Showcasing Your Company

If you have a number of openings for a particular position (for example, a salesperson), I recommend inviting the applicants who survived the initial screening to a recruitment evening. To further refine the list of applicants, require that they wear name tags so that you can take note of anybody who stands out during the evening, either positively or negatively. Some people will eliminate themselves after learning more about the position, and some may present themselves poorly, so you'll be able to eliminate them.

The benefits of such an evening are threefold: It will test the desire of the potential recruits to find out more about your company and the role for which they applied. It will give you a chance to thoroughly examine each candidate's attentiveness, personal presentation, and attitude. And it will offer an opportunity for your leaders to be involved in the recruitment process by participating as presenters at this session.

I have run these evenings previously with great success by incorporating the following agenda items: the history of the company, the company's vision and values, its strategic game plan, its focus on people development, an overview of the position, an explanation of compensation (if you are comfortable explaining this before going through the interview stage), the tools of the position, a description of a day in the position, and questions for the presenters.

My recommendation is that these presentations be a maximum of ninety minutes long. Involving leaders who will manage the candidates chosen and a person currently in the position (when possible) will help in the success of these evenings. Do not oversell the company or the position. Be honest about all aspects of the position so people know what they are signing up for. This will help guard against people becoming disillusioned with the position soon after they start.

❻ The Interview

You should go into the interview process prepared with a clear set of questions that you intend to ask each candidate and a clear process for evaluating them during an interview. That said, no matter how much we plan and structure an interview for empirical evaluation, in the end, interviewing is an art that takes years to master. I recommend having a seasoned interviewer take part in the process. He will see or probe for attributes, skills, and potential problems that a novice might overlook.

Before the actual interview, I favor asking the applicants to perform a task, such as preparing a one-page description of themselves, writing up an overview of the industry and what attracts them to it, or preparing a description of some of the things that they have achieved in their lives of which they are proud. Asking them to perform a task like this before the interview will give you a guide to their attitudes and show how keen they are to obtain the role.

Overall, I prefer a behavioral approach to interviewing. Behavioral interviewing involves asking about an experience when the applicant believes she demonstrated the particular skill or attribute under discussion. Seek a clear answer that describes her actions and the outcome of the situation. Ask follow-up questions until you can effectively evaluate how well the skill was displayed. Give her sufficient time to recall and describe a previous event that pertains to the inquiry. Find out what she learned from the situation. Have different backup questions that probe the same skills in case an applicant cannot think of a situation that fits the initial query. Many times the past can predict future behavior, but future behavior may be altered by lessons learned in the past, whether positive or negative.

The key throughout the whole recruitment/selection process, and particularly the interview process, is to find out who the applicants are, not what they know. People can be taught skills, but not basic behavioral or personality traits. Keep in mind the old adage "Hire for attitude; train for skill." Following are some interview tips to keep you trained on this goal and to help you identify some key questions to ask:

- Focus on achievements, not fancy résumés.

- Examine applicants' track records very closely. Why did they leave previous employers? Does their history show growth and progressive responsibility? What did they enjoy or dislike about prior positions?

- Pay close attention to their dress and grooming. Are their nails clean, their shoes free of dirt, their clothes pressed, and their general appearance of a high professional standard? Remember, they are in an interview process, trying to impress you, and this will be the best you see them present themselves. They should be putting their best foot forward.

- Be aware of their behavior during the interview. Are they overwhelmed? How do they handle stressful situations? Do they keep interrupting you?

- Get a glimpse of their communication skills. Are their answers directly related to the question? Are their responses concise or do they talk excessively? Are they good listeners? Do not pay

attention to past job descriptions; ask them what they learned
and what they achieved.

- Focus on specific projects and dig deep on past results.

- Ask the question "If I met your previous boss socially, what
would he/she say about you?"

- Determine if they have a problem with authority. How do they
discuss their relationships with previous bosses?

- Determine if they are team players. Did they interact well with
their peers? Do they use "I" or "we" when they discuss previous results?

- Find out what their expectations are and the type of environment they like to work in. Discover how they prefer to be man-
aged. They may have great skills, but if a candidate is looking
for structured guidance and the position calls for significant
autonomy, then he is not a good match for the position.

- Involve some of their potential peers to talk with them and
obtain feedback.

- The hiring process is a two-way street: You should not only be
looking for a candidate to match the position, you should also
be sure that your company and the position are a match for the
person. Ask them why the company and position are a good fit
for them. Probe for credible and authentic reasons. Do their
values match the organizational values?

- Before you make an offer, send the candidate to lunch with
a trusted employee to see the real person, not the interview
person.

IT IS YOUR responsibility to ensure that all people involved in recruitment are fully trained in the recruiting process. This includes making sure they are aware of antidiscrimination laws and the legal ramifications of asking about applicants' personal lives and some areas of past employment. These restrictions differ from state to state and country to country. Ensure that your selection process is fair, professional, and always closely followed. Be very clear that deviation from the process *will not* be tolerated.

BE CREATIVE ABOUT RETENTION

If you've followed my prescriptions so far, you've gone through the effort to recruit the right people and ensure that you're paying them fairly. Now you have to figure out how to keep them, and keep them happy. Money is not the only factor determining an employee's contentment. Contentment also comes from feeling valued, respected, recognized, and acknowledged for hard work. Over the years, I have conducted retention interviews with my people and have developed the following list of reasons for why they stay. These ten points have been confirmed by many other researchers as compelling reasons why people do not leave.

❶ Career opportunities, training, and development

❷ Exciting and challenging work

❸ Fair remuneration

❹ Supportive leaders

❺ Feeling of community

❻ Feeling valued and respected

❼ Excellent communication

❽ Great culture and environment

❾ Able to make a difference

❿ Pride in the organization and products

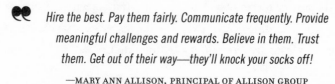

Hire the best. Pay them fairly. Communicate frequently. Provide meaningful challenges and rewards. Believe in them. Trust them. Get out of their way—they'll knock your socks off!
—MARY ANN ALLISON, PRINCIPAL OF ALLISON GROUP

So what is the bottom line to employee retention, the element that runs through most of these factors? SUPERVISION! The quality of the supervision that an employee receives is critical to employee retention. People leave their managers more often than they leave their companies.

People want to know that what they do is being noticed and appreciated. In fact, many people hold on to letters of praise from their bosses for years, long after they've left a job or cleaned out their files. I know I do! The reason that supervision is so crucial is because effective, authentic leadership is the only way to make employees feel special. This book is all about developing your people and making them feel special. Employees who feel valuable, supported, appreciated, paid fairly for their skills, coached, and developed will be very unlikely to leave the organization.

Lab Work

A twenty-five-year Gallup Organization study conducted interviews with 12 million workers from more than 7,000 companies and found that their relationship with their manager largely determined how long they would stay.

Watson Wyatt conducted a 2005/2006 Communications ROI study of 335 U.S. and Canadian companies. The research defined effective communication in several ways, such as helping employees understand the business; exhibiting strong leadership skills, especially during organizational change; and explaining and promoting new policies and programs. Companies that scored in the top third for effective communication had a market premium (market value exceeding cost of assets) 19.4 percent higher than the average of companies in the survey; they were 4.5 times more likely to exhibit employee engagement; and they were 20 percent less likely to lose employees to other companies (Krell, 2006).

Nine Tips for Enhancing Retention

If you, your company, or one of your leaders has a concern with retention, following these tips will ensure that employee retention is improved. These ideas are not all-embracing; there will be other things that you could be doing as well to enhance retention. But if you aren't doing the things on this list, you should start here.

❶ Create a Sound Initiation Process

Be prepared for new hires: have business cards printed, their work area outfitted, phone and computer ready to go, and a plan/layout of the office prepared with the names of other employees on their work areas. This is a great way of saying "welcome to the team" and displaying efficiency and professionalism. Go the extra mile.

Choose mentors for all new recruits, and try to match the mentors to the new employees' personalities. Introduce mentors prior to the new employees' start dates via email. Also ensure that a new employee's mentor is there to meet her on her first day. Mentoring is critical to assist a new recruit in settling in quickly and learning the business with the minimum of fuss. Be very careful selecting mentors, and ensure that they are well matched to the recruit, briefed on expectations, and rewarded for their successes. Obtain feedback from the mentor daily and also meet with the new recruit daily for at least the first two weeks.

Show new employees they are valuable by doing thirty-, sixty-, and ninety-day follow-ups. Assign new employees to leaders two levels up from their position. The leader should approach the employee and hold a fifteen-to-twenty-minute meeting to see how their training, mentoring, and experience on the job are going at each of the thirty-day intervals. Help them solve the problems of being the new kid on the block. You will be amazed what an impact this small gesture has on retaining new employees. Establishing a caring environment right at the beginning of the relationship can have lasting results.

New employee care is the responsibility of the entire organization. The establishment of a welcoming and open environment to retain new hires is everyone's responsibility, and retention factors can be built right into bonus systems for leaders. You can also give existing employees a stake in helping new employees get acclimated and feel valued by tying a department or business unit's employee bonus to its turnover rate and/or its ability to hold on to new employees.

❷ Create a Job Enrichment Program

Energize your people by looking at what they do and how they do it. Involve them in finding creative and innovative ways to enhance their roles and the processes involved. An enriched job will

- encourage creativity and initiative;
- allow an employee to set her own individual and team objectives;
- stop boredom from setting in;
- give greater autonomy and a sense of freedom;
- encourage employees to learn new skills;
- allow contact with clients to enable processes to become customer focused; and
- let employees know exactly where they fit in the process, giving them a sense of community.

❸ Conduct Retention Interviews and Gather Retention Statistics

Do you know what your employees' compelling reasons to stay are? If not, you need to ask them as the first step in enhancing your retention. Many companies do exit interviews, but few do retention interviews. It is far more important to find out what your people like and dislike about their roles before they decide to leave than when they have already decided to leave. Conduct these interviews with a range of your people and all of your top performers to really find out what is making them stay and what may be making them consider leaving.

If you are just starting to conduct retention interviews, you will need to ask employees what they like and dislike about the organization. An excellent way to do this is to conduct a "Stop/Start/Continue" exercise, where you ask them, "To make this a better place to work, what should we stop doing, start doing, and continue doing?" Additionally, ask questions like the following:

- If you could change one thing in your area, what would it be?
- Would you recommend your job to a friend? Why or why not?
- If you left, what would you miss?

Most companies create a turnover analysis to determine why people are leaving. Instead, create retention statistics. How many people were hired in the last year? How many new people were successful in retaining their position in that year? For two or three years? How many people were moved to new higher-level, same-level, and lower-level positions? What was the number of employees completing orientations, probationary periods, or volunteer training sessions? How many dollars did the department save the company by retaining recently hired employees? Create an accurate and effective scorecard for all leaders that keeps tabs on their abilities to retain new hires and promote existing employees into their desired positions.

When you know the compelling retention factors and statistics in your particular business, you need to become innovative and put solutions in place to aid retention.

❹ Have Career Conversations

Don't be afraid of conducting career interviews. This is an excellent chance to get to know more about your employee and for her to understand what skills she may need to acquire to achieve the role she desires. The key to success in these sessions is preparation, asking plenty of questions and listening intently to the answers. Find out about the following, and then prompt her to ensure that you clearly understand what she has said:

- Where do you see yourself in six months, one year, and three years?
- What are your unique assets?
- What do you value most about your current role and business?
- Where do you see your development needs, and what can we do to assist you in that development?

Throughout the career conversations, provide specific feedback with examples and obtain your employee's views. You should also give plenty of encouragement and support so that she feels as comfortable as possible. At the end of the conversation, ensure that an action plan is put in place, developed, and agreed upon by all concerned.

❺ Keep Employees in the Loop

Keep your employees aware of things that are happening in your business and industry. Trust them with important information and they'll feel valued and protected. There are times when leaders fear that their people cannot be told what is really going on within the business. In my opinion, these times should be rare. Most leaders would be surprised by the ability of their team members to handle sensitive or potentially negative information. And often they'll offer insight or suggestions that are helpful.

Often leaders will hoard information to keep their teams working and focused and to protect productivity. This often works against them, because there is usually a leak of information and

Lab Work

A Mercer Human Resources consulting survey of 2,600 people showed that only 15 percent who enjoy strong workplace communications are thinking of seeking new jobs, compared with 41 percent at organizations lacking communication.

your people feel let down because their leaders didn't trust them and share the information with them directly. On the other hand, if a leader shares information early and honestly and as openly as possible, employees feel trusted, important, and valued, and any productivity drop is minimized. The grapevine is alive and well in all organizations. Be the first voice so that this informal stream of communication never carries a surprise! Try the following:

- Take people for a coffee chat where you share your thoughts on the business and the industry. This gains you enormous respect, and they will also open up to tell you what they are feeling about their roles and their future career prospects.

- Conduct focus group functions to keep employees abreast of company news and industry changes. Invite employees from different departments to create relationships that reach throughout the company. Focus groups can be used in a variety of ways. They can help you keep your ear to the grapevine and explain away issues before they fester, ask about ways to boost employee morale, or share views on management. Invite different employees each session and make them feel important by involving them and listening to them, instead of merely telling them what is happening.

■ Create an employee newsletter. Let employees contribute or write editorials on various subjects pertaining to the work environment. If the newsletter is interesting, informative, helpful, and fun, employees will look forward to each publication.

❻ Be Family Friendly

Life demands have increased exponentially over recent years. Your worker will most likely want to be able to share the home workload. If you do not offer the following benefits your people desire, they will not have to look far for an employer who will:

■ Flexible work hours

■ Maternity and paternity programs

■ Childcare assistance

■ Rewards involving family

■ Time off to attend family activities

■ Option to work from home

Be creative and involve your team members in brainstorming ideas that will make them and their families feel great about your sensitivity to family. You will find that their ideas will not be outlandish, and the opportunity to put their thoughts forward will make them feel valued. A word of caution: treat all ideas seriously and put in place a follow-up action plan that keeps everyone informed. If an idea will not work, sit down with the proposing employee and sincerely explain the obstacles. Aim to reach another solution together that will be feasible for all.

❼ Engender Respect

Read Prescription 1, and remember to treat your team members with respect and dignity if you want them to stay.

❽ Value Your People

Read Prescriptions 1 and 2 and the next section on recognizing your valuable team members. Remember to show your people consistently that they are valued, cared for, and essential to your team.

❾ Recognize and Reward Their Contributions

Read the next two sections on recognition and reward!

RECOGNIZE YOUR VALUABLE TEAM MEMBERS

After twenty years, I still vividly recall the excitement of receiving an award at an annual company conference in front of senior management and 150 of my peers, all top performers who qualified for the conference. My name was called and flashed onto huge screens with "Number 3 in National Production" beneath it. I strode over the red carpet to the stage, where our CEO and the bank president presented a fabulous trophy to me. Then our picture was taken, and I received a significant cash prize. That feeling of appreciation, recognition, and reward will last forever. The trophy and the photo still represent feelings of pride and accomplishment. The cash is long gone!

The manager thinks people want to feel important. The leader knows people need to feel significant. And recognition is a major factor in helping people to feel significant. Being noticed for our efforts and given some recognition for our contribution is a major motivator, and creating a positive motivational mood among your team is a key to getting people to follow your leadership. Yet many leaders do not realize the power they can generate through simple acts of recognition. Think back to your best boss or schoolteacher. Why was she the best? Most likely it is because of the way she made you feel.

Look for creative ways to recognize everyone on your team. Be innovative. Involve your people and come up with unique ways to regularly recognize them. Leaders need to be sincere, operating authentically from their hearts, because if you are disingenuous when recognizing people, it is blatantly obvious and will do untold harm. Follow this advice and watch your team's contentment and commitment to the company soar.

Give Daily Recognition

There are many ways to ensure that you and your team can create a habit of daily recognition. Here are some options for you to select from:

- Put five sticky-tab flags on the right side of the telephone, transferring one to the left each time you recognize someone.

- Put five coins in your pocket and transfer one to the other pocket for each recognition act.

- Keep five recognition cards on your desk and make sure they aren't there at the end of a day.

- Create a section in your weekly planner that lists people to praise, and cross off the names as you catch them doing something right.

- Leave voice-mail messages on cell phones praising their efforts. They will play these messages for their family and friends.

Create a program that works for you and stick to it. I recognize at least five people daily and use the "sticky-tab" routine.

Praise Specifically

When giving praise, do not generalize; make it specific and meaningful. Telling people they are doing a good job is not going to make them stay. For praise to help with retention, it needs to be heartfelt and specific. Develop your own openers, remembering that sincerity is the key. Here are a few to get you started:

- One of the things I really enjoy about you is your attitude. I love it when . . .

- The work you are doing on project X is excellent.

- You really made a difference when . . .

- It really made my day getting a call from a delighted customer who said . . .

- This project could not have been successful without you doing . . .

- You set a great example for the team when you . . .

Remember, praise in public; offer constructive criticism in private!

Recognize Appropriate Behavior

Don't just recognize the top performers. Top performances certainly need to be recognized, but use praise to emphasize the type of behavior you want people to emulate. Once again, in words from *The One-Minute Manager,* "Catch someone doing something right and tell them about it." In addition to top performances, recognize individual and team bests, positive behavioral changes, and top efforts from new people.

Contact Your Top Performers Regularly

Create an environment of high morale and positive motivation by building the self-esteem of your people. One way to do this is for high-level leaders to contact the company's top performers in a personal way each month. For instance, the CEO could regularly call or write a personal note to the standout performers. This is a great thing to commit to and will boost morale and retention.

If you decide to send letters to your top performers, do not fall into the trap of sending form letters. Your top people will receive these often and just see this as something typed up by your assistant. Be sure that the praise is specific, relevant, and accurate. When I was a salesperson, I was fortunate enough to be a top-ten performer on a consistent basis. Our leader at the time would send a typed letter acknowledging superior performance to each member of the monthly top ten: "Congratulations, Ken, your performance last month was outstanding. Number 3 in the country with sales of $65,000 is something to be proud of. It is the performance of people like you that drives this company."

The first time I received this letter, I thought it was nice. But the positive effect of these form letters wore off. I recall talking to other top performers and they felt the same way. We felt the recognition was shallow. Then, one month I received the same letter telling me how proud I must have been about my performance. The funny thing was that my achievement, by my standards, was very ordinary that month.

I called our leader and told him that I felt I should let him know that I wasn't proud of my previous month's performance; in fact, I told him this was my worst month in the past year and I was revisiting the basics to get myself back on track. He didn't really listen to me, saying, "Well you were still in the top ten," and he did not change his approach to recognition.

That day I vowed that when I was a leader, no matter how many people were on the team, I would seek out superior performance and recognize it creatively and personally. I would recognize my employees in a way that showed I really knew what was happening with their performance.

Know exactly what is going on and forward handwritten cards acknowledging this. For example, if one of your top performers has a month below their usual par and there is a reason, such as family illness or moving, acknowledge this in your card. Keep a register of whom you send cards to, and if you are using motivational-type cards, record what type was sent to avoid sending the same card the next month. Also, do not restrict these cards to your top performers. Include great efforts from rookies, administrators, and people who have had a tough month due to external issues. Remember, be a good finder!

Send monthly cards to at least 20 percent of your team. Yes, it takes around four hours monthly, but I can tell you that you cannot do anything more important in those four hours than sending these personal cards.

 The glory of friendship is not in the outstretched hand, nor *the kindly smile, nor the joy of companionship; it is in the spiritual inspiration that comes to one when he discovers that someone else believes in him and is willing to trust him.*
—RALPH WALDO EMERSON, AUTHOR, POET, AND PHILOSOPHER

Involve the Family

Respecting the values and responsibilities of employees in your company who have families and really caring about them will reward you tenfold with loyalty and commitment. Send a card home praising a hardworking employee and acknowledging the support his or her family provides. Include a surprise with this card, such as movie tickets, a dinner voucher, or another treat your employees can share with their partners.

Roll up Your Sleeves and Show Support

While this may not seem like recognition, it is recognition of a special kind—recognition that your employees are working hard and could use a hand. Always show your employees that you are not afraid to roll up your sleeves and help with their work when they are struggling. Let them know that you are all in it together; that kind of support and recognition is one of the best ways to develop trust and credibility. If you are not sure how to solve a problem, find someone who can assist them right away so that your employees know that you care about the problems they face and are there to help when they are at a loss. Help when it is needed, but don't overdo it. Let employees reach for and solve challenging problems within their grasp.

 Every single person you meet has a sign around his or her
neck that says "Make Me Feel Important." If you can do that,
you'll be a success not only in business but in life as well.
—MARY KAY ASH, FOUNDER OF MARY KAY COSMETICS, INC.

REWARD YOUR VALUABLE TEAM MEMBERS

Developing a solid reward program is a key way to create a positive environment and make employees feel appreciated and significant. The wonderful thing about rewards is the flexibility and creativity you can employ when designing them. No matter what the needs or motivators of your employees, you can offer rewards that will improve your retention levels.

One mistake that many managers make is to assume that rewards are all about money. While money is a key motivator for many, a feeling of recognition and significance is often as or more important. So before we delve into the specifics of building a great rewards program, here are a few basic guidelines to consider:

- Ensure that your compensation is fair before introducing rewards. Small rewards can seem like cheap efforts to buy loyalty if compensation is below industry standards.

- Reward more than just top performers; reward rookies, personal bests, and any type of behavior you want to encourage in others.

- Make sure your rewards are not seen as entitlements. If they are easily earned or if everybody gets them, then they aren't doing their intended job of highlighting and promoting very specific behaviors.

- Offer a simple merit-based reward system for all employees who meet certain standards, such as standards set for exceptional customer service, exceptional contribution to the company, or exceptional work quality.

- Beware of only providing cash rewards; be innovative and think of other ways to reward employees.

- Tailor rewards to what your people desire; if you aren't sure what they value, do a survey.

- Offer a choice of reward when possible; remember that different things motivate different people.

- Incorporate family into the reward when possible and appropriate.

- Be creative and have fun when rewarding employees; if you are having fun, they will have fun.

- Make sure rewards are immediate and sincere. The delivery should be as close as possible to the specific related event or achievement. Also remember that if the leader delivering the reward is not respected or viewed as sincere, the reward will mean almost nothing.

In my opinion the following leadership principle sums up the power of recognition and reward:

> **The Greatest Leadership Principle on Earth**
> People do what you reward.
> They do not do
> What you want for
> What you wish for
> What you hope for.
> They do what you reward! (Leboeuf, 1985)

Competitions

Create competitions to drive desired behaviors. People have egos, and the recognition of being a winner is more important than the prize. These competitions should be individual, team based, and company based. They can boost morale, increase production, and

🧪 Lab Work

According to the "Top Five Total Rewards Priorities" survey (from Deloitte Consulting LLP's Human Capital Practice and the International Society of Certified Employee Benefit Specialists), the priority of reward programs that attract new employees and motivate existing employees rose in 2005. This was the first time in the eleven-year history of the survey that attracting and retaining employees through rewards programs has rated this high.

A study conducted in 2005 by the National Association for Employee Recognition showed that 83 percent of companies used special events to motivate employees. Gift cards were used 74 percent of the time, and 64 percent of employees were given merchandise incentives to acknowledge workers' efforts. Trips and travel were only employed 15 percent of the time ("Top Tools for Motivation," *Incentive*, 2005).

develop passion, and they are just plain fun! All of these competitions can also be used to make a fast start to a plan year or a traditionally slow month.

Individual competitions can be run over a six-to-eight-week period to ensure that competitors maintain focus.

- Have weekly updates via your internal newsletter.
- If you have a superior performer who consistently wins these competitions, have the major prize as a "lucky draw," with entries allocated toward the final draw for achieving certain levels on a weekly basis.

- Have a rookie award in the competition for employees with fewer than six months of service but who show considerable promise.

- Individuals who do not meet business quality standards should not be eligible for prizes.

One individual competition that I had was called "The Newcombe Award," which was named after a salesperson on our team who had met or exceeded the weekly sales goal for fifty-two weeks straight. The trophy was first given to employees when targets were met for ten straight weeks, with points also allocated to spend in a corporate gift catalog. Notation was made on the trophy, and further rewards points were given when targets were met or exceeded for twenty, thirty, forty, and fifty consecutive weeks, allowing grace for any weeks on leave. The Newcombe Award became treasured and drove our people to ensure that they met their weekly target, as missing a week dropped them back to the starting point.

Team-based competitions should be run for longer periods than individual competitions. Setting up team-based competitions on your financial quarters can be effective.

- Prizes for team-based competitions should be linked to company goals over the period of the competition. If company goals are exceeded during the competition, prizes can be doubled.

- Base the competition on something that can be tallied week by week whenever possible so that teams can track their scores as time goes by.

- Offer weekly updates in your internal newsletter; try having an anonymous tipster predict the outcome of next week's tallies.

- Try using a format in which individual teams compete against each other directly each week in some way, such as a trivia competition about your products or services. This can be a fun learning experience and will work well if what you are tracking is not related to numbers (for example, sales).

■ You can break your team into subteams and use similar tactics. Be sure you have varying levels of performers on each team.

While individual and team competitions can be great, they can also take employees' eyes off the bigger picture of company performance. Use company-based competitions to recognize different levels of winning and to emphasize that your company is competing in the business world. Ensure that you drive home the "our company vs. the rest" mentality by letting your people know how you are faring within your industry. Everyone should know how the company is performing against the monthly plan. Celebrate successes with a morning tea, coffee break, or some similar event every time the company achieves a monthly, quarterly, or annual plan.

Awards

Aside from competitions, offering employees awards that are based on the nominations and votes of their peers is also a good idea. These awards may be more related to attitude or certain skills than specific goal achievements—for instance, you could offer an award for the most helpful or caring employee, the most fun to work with, or whatever else you think of. It's a great way to show employees that they are valued by their peers.

Newsletters

Distribute weekly and monthly newsletters that are interesting, inspirational, educational, and motivational. Include in these newsletters the names of standout employees, team status on monthly goals, tips from top performers or specialists from a certain department (remember the development plans from Prescription 1), product and company updates or enhancements, the top-achieving rookies, and competition updates.

If you create these newsletters in the right way, employees will look forward to receiving them. In my situation we had Thursday deadlines to ensure that the newsletter was emailed out before close of business on Friday. The team leaders longed to receive it because it included their team rankings in order of performance for the week. And team members loved to see their names on the list of top performers.

Monthly Achievers Breakfast or Lunch

As a leader, consider hosting a monthly breakfast or lunch attended by people performing at a set standard in that particular month. If specific performance is difficult to measure in your department, choose one person who you believe offered the greatest contribution and then have other team members nominate other people to attend. If you have other leaders reporting to you, have them each nominate one person from their team.

As with all of these events, when you are taking people away from their work, you need to ensure that they are receiving value in the form of education, motivation, or inspiration to make it worth their while to attend. At the lunch, have people share ideas for the team or company, but also relax and have fun. Select random business cards for a drawing to win movie tickets, wine, or chocolates.

Monthly Meetings

Conduct a monthly team meeting, preferably off-site. These meetings need to be inspirational, educational, and motivational. Here are some issues that need to be covered in these meetings:

- Awards and presentations for competitions, top performers, and others

- Certificates for personal bests, as long as the bests are above a certain benchmark

- Customer testimonials—read any communication the team or individuals received from customers

- Best practice sessions—have a few top achievers talk for five or ten minutes about what habits or practices they use

- Company and team performance updates—let your team know how they are doing and how the company is doing compared to the plan, for the month and for the year

- Updates on existing competitions and launch new competitions

- New product or policy launches

- External speakers (occasionally)

These meetings should not last longer than two hours; keep them snappy, but professional, and have fun. If you are having any difficulty with attendance, examine the content and how these meetings are conducted. Are they interesting? Helpful? Motivating? If not, fix it. No one wants to attend a lifeless meeting. It does not matter if your team is a group of self-employed contractors. If your meetings are motivational and add value, attendance will be high. In one of my previous roles, all of our people were self-employed contractors, and attendance at the sales meetings, although not compulsory, was still always well over 90 percent because the meetings were meaningful and stimulating.

Conferences

Qualifying for a conference is an immense driver for many workers. The conference does not have to be somewhere exotic or extravagant, but it does need to be light, fun, educational, and motivating. The following is a list of tips for a successful conference:

- Set challenging benchmarks to secure attendance, aiming to have your top 15–20 percent qualify.

- Set benchmarks for leaders to qualify as well.

- Have the top 10 percent who qualify bring a partner.

- Send tantalizers to your people's home address in the months and weeks leading up to the conference (a postcard showing a resort, a bottle of sand, or something relating to the location of the conference).

- Keep business sessions short and sharp and presented mainly by attendees.

- Have plenty of fun activities.

- Once again, make it educational, motivational, and inspirational.

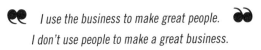

I use the business to make great people. I don't use people to make a great business.

—RALPH STAYER, FOUNDER OF WISCONSIN SAUSAGE COMPANY

DIAGNOSIS: BORING REWARDS
THAT DON'T INSPIRE LOYALTY

If your rewards don't promote anything but a yawn and a halfhearted "thanks," chances are you're not tapping into what your people really want.

Here's a list of cures for your ailing rewards program:

- Offer household items, which can be powerful as a constant reminder of achievement.

- Family weekends away acknowledge support from home as well as superior performance—so do tickets to a theme park or other family-based activity.

- A person who achieves consistently can be offered the flexibility to set his own schedule. He will not let you down . . . and this flexibility will inspire others.

- Praise exceptional performances in front of the standout worker's peers. Public praise is powerful. But keep this for truly excellent results, or you risk watering down its power.

- Tickets to an educational seminar or reimbursement of tuition will appeal to people motivated by personal growth. You could also offer personal development books or tapes. (In my time as a leader, I have given away more than five hundred books . . . more than two hundred were *The One-Minute Manager!*)

- Send a gift to a partner or spouse who has clearly offered your employee a lot of support, particularly during very busy or stressful work periods.

- When an excellent employee is on vacation, contact her toward the end of her holiday and surprise her by offering an extra day off. Ensure that she realizes this is a bonus day that is not coming out of her current entitlement balance.

- Annually allocate five days per twenty employees and allow employees to nominate colleagues for a "Reward Day." When an employee achieves ten reward-day nominations, he receives a day off.

- Create "Time Off Chips." These are a great way to say "well done." You do not need to give heaps of time off, but make chips for an extra hour at lunch, a few hours in the morning, or a half day, and they will work very well.

CREATING CONTENTED EMPLOYEES who will stay with your team and company for the long term is not a complicated process; it just takes the right amount of attention to making sure you have the right people in the right positions, that you're meeting people's basic compensation expectations, and that you are dedicated to recognizing and rewarding employees specifically and personally.

YOUR NEW HEALTH REGIMEN

Develop a well-designed recruitment and hiring process that focuses on making sure you've got the right people in the right positions.

Focus on establishing fair and competitive salary packages first and then enhance this with creative rewards and incentives that wow your employees.

Follow the ten basic steps to retaining your valued employees.

Recognize the little things employees do to improve sales, service, production, etc., not just the big achievements or the top performers.

Praise employees specifically and every day.

Show recognition by being supportive and lending a hand.

Be creative, innovative, and flexible in how you recognize and reward employees. Remember that individuals are motivated by different things.

Use competitions, meetings, newsletters, conferences, and other ways of connecting in a timely and sincere way with employees to praise and reward them.

Motivate, inspire, educate—and have fun!

PRESCRIPTION 4

THE CURE FOR EMPLOYEES
WHO UNDERPERFORM

ADDRESSING ISSUES OF poor performance is a challenge for most leaders. We all want to believe that if we create the right environment, provide employees with the right tools, and offer good training and development opportunities, we'll never have to talk to an employee about poor performance. It makes us uncomfortable just thinking about it.

But the reality is that no matter what you do to ensure high performance levels, not every person on your team is going to live up to your or your organization's expectations. And while pulling an employee up to higher levels of performance may not be a part of your job that you look forward to, it can be a highly rewarding experience for both of you. But if you want to be successful, you have to have a process and plan for how to deal with issues of performance.

That's why my fourth prescription is:

R̽ If you want to have employees performing at top levels, or even expected levels, you have to set high expectations and live by them, review performance constantly, address and analyze performance deviation immediately and directly, and coach, train, and support poor performers until they've improved.

SET HIGH EXPECTATIONS

No matter what kind of standards you set as a leader—high, low, or in between—your people will take them as their goal. If you set high standards, they will strive to achieve them. If you set low standards, they will aim only for those easy targets. You have the power to establish the standard and the tone of employee performance. Employees will follow your lead. If you think excellent performance is important, so will the members of your team.

Some employees will feel that a mediocre performance is all they need to offer to keep their jobs. A leader cannot accept mediocre effort. Even 80 percent effort should be abominable to you. Be sure to emphasize and demonstrate your seriousness about the standards you set by holding yourself and everyone on your team to these standards, and don't hide the fact that achieving mediocre results will have repercussions.

The following numbers represent a typical team before there is a commitment to personal development plans and a focus on positive performance management:

- 20 percent high achievers

- 60 percent average achievers

- 20 percent nonachievers

Where is the minimum acceptable performance for this team? Most leaders will say in the middle. Wrong! The minimum acceptable level is what the lowest nonachiever is attaining. He is still on the team, and all team members will view their performance as acceptable to you. You have to set a high standard and enforce it, or the standard of the lowest performer will be the standard you are actually setting in the minds of your team members.

Your most important expectation of all should always be constant improvement. You must demand it and support it in every way you can. This doesn't mean you should neglect radical change in some areas of your business, just don't expect people development changes to happen overnight. You cannot simultaneously work on enhancing all people's strengths and eradicating any weaknesses you

 Lab Work

In their book *Discover Your Sales Strengths* (Warner Books, 2003), Benson Smith and Tony Rutigliano write: "In the course of our work we have studied sales forces for some of the best companies, companies that have carefully recruited and selected their representatives. Even in the best companies, we found that 35 percent of the sales force did not have the talents necessary to achieve acceptable results predictably. This rather considerable group—one of every three salespeople out there—is consistently in the bottom half of the performance curve."

see. Rather, you have to concentrate on gradually capitalizing on the strengths of individuals and taking these to a new level, isolating any weaknesses that are threatening, and working on these as well. Following are some tips for setting and achieving high standards within your team:

- Tie performance standards directly to the organization's strategic goals and objectives.

- When setting expectations, be honest, courageous, ethical, consistent, and focused on results.

- Involve the team and obtain input before setting the standards.

- Model the standards you've established.

- Reward people who exceed the standards.

- Remember that once you've set the standards, it's your responsibility to remove any obstacles your employees face in meeting them.

- Build and maintain a positive environment.

- Hold a meeting with key leaders and establish a plan and detailed program for how new standards will be met and how improvement will be achieved.

- Accept no excuses, but value truthful, valid, and clear explanations.

- When stepping into a new role, take some time to engage your people, engendering trust and respect while inspecting performance. Once you've learned the terrain, act decisively to set clear, high standards.

- Make sure the standards are consistent across the team or organization.

- Refuse to carry passengers—address substandard performance immediately and fairly.

In my early days as a manager, I led a sales team of financial planners working out of bank branches. We were failing to meet expectations. I knew that our group had the makings of an excellent team, but our current substandard performance called for some shock treatment. Research with our bank colleagues revealed the unthinkable: we were expecting the bankers to refer their prized customers to us, but we had members of our team who the bankers didn't trust.

After an extended process of due diligence to unearth the truth, I dismissed a number of salespeople who had entirely lost the trust of their bank colleagues. I also put the bottom 20 percent of our sales force as well as two of our leaders on performance counseling, with a focus on improving both attitude and skills. The intention was to have our team leaders diligently work with these people to bring them up to required standard.

The success of this "Rehabilitate or Release" program is shown in the fact that 60 percent of the employees and one of the leaders being counseled turned their performance around to become valuable employees who met their objectives. One of the salespeople not only turned his sales performance around but also later went on to become a leader—one of the most successful in our business, who now runs his own training and development company.

The program also served as a wake-up call for mid-level performers. These people realized that violating the trust necessary for bank referrals or "picking the low-hanging fruit" would not be tolerated. They also realized that, with the bottom 20 percent of the old sales team being rehabilitated or released, they might now become the bottom group; this motivated them to lift their performances. Also, there was a sharp lift in attitude in response to the clear message that no matter the level of performance, a poor attitude or loss of the trust of bank colleagues would not be tolerated. The fact that leaders were not exempt from the performance scrutiny gave credibility to the process. And the team performance lifted to such an extent that they clearly won the award for the number-one team in the country.

As the leader, you hold the success of your organization in your hand. If everyone is performing at or above the standards you've set, there is no way the organization should not meet its established goals.

REVIEW PERFORMANCE CONSTANTLY

Reviewing the performance of your team and team members is not something that you, as an authentic leader, should do once a year, once a quarter, or once a month. It is something you do every single day, all the time. This may sound time consuming, but it isn't. It comes naturally with the effort you put into connecting with your team and focusing on results. And it is your responsibility as a leader, because the performance of individuals and teams drives all organizational success.

Of course a leader needs to have a helicopter view of what is happening in the business, but he also needs to keep a close eye on the details. Staying close to your operation and keeping a deep understanding of your team and the issues they face daily without micromanaging is difficult, to say the least. But if you set clear expectations, communicate with your team regularly, and try to be an authentic leader, your team will respect your attention and realize that your close observation is an effort to understand their situations and help them, not to micromanage or check up on them. Regularly gauging and discussing performance levels with employees will keep you aware of what they're achieving and establish the importance of the team's goals in your people's minds and hearts.

When you always address performance issues in the right way, your employees will respond to and maintain the standards you set. Accountability will become a part of your culture. Without active performance management, your written rules will mean nothing. Later in this prescription we will look at performance management and how you can get a clear understanding of why people are not meeting performance expectations and what they need in terms of skill and behavioral development (see Prescriptions 1 and 2).

Watch and Learn

I think the following might be one of the greatest leadership principles of all time:

When assessing performance, do not listen to what people say, watch what they do.

This is how you review performance regularly and informally: you watch what your team members do.

- Walk around and observe your team members working. Talk to people; it will become evident who the respected workers are.

- Develop a keen understanding of each department's role in the overall process.

- Meet weekly with team members to examine performance against goals.

- Ask questions to drill down and find the real explanations.

- Remember *The One-Minute Manager* rule: "Catch someone doing something right and tell them about it."

Develop a Thorough Performance Appraisal Process

A professional and well-planned performance appraisal process is the capstone of a consistent and thorough focus on performance. It serves multiple purposes, including clearly communicating to employees how their performance is viewed, giving employees an opportunity to address concerns directly, creating an opportunity to establish long-term development and career goals, and creating a written record of performance issues for human resource and legal purposes.

A note of caution, however: A yearly or biannual performance review should be a written confirmation of months of performance

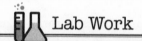 Lab Work

The Institute for Corporate Productivity conducted a survey of more than a thousand organizations in the United States. The organizations ranged in size from those with fewer than one hundred employees to those with more than ten thousand. The findings were startling. Only 8 percent of respondents felt that their company's performance management system actually contributed to individual improvement. Almost half—47 percent—were not sure if their performance management process made any contribution at all. Seventy percent of the participants found that the process lacked consistency across the organization; some managers and departments were better or worse than others. Only 36 percent of respondents found performance management "essential." These results are alarming (Oakes, 2007).

discussions and actions, not the one time you connect with employees about their performance. If the review process leaves employees surprised, then performance is not being observed, rewarded, or addressed in a regular and consistent way.

Generic Seven-Step "No Surprises" Appraisal Process

Every company and culture is different, and the performance appraisal process has to reflect the unique aspects of the organization. Will you tie raises to the appraisal process? Will you use self-evaluation as part of the appraisal process? Will you use a rating system? These are just a few of the questions you and your leadership team or your human resources department will need to address as you develop your system.

❶ **Have an attributes/skills development system in place.** All people should be working on developing a selected attribute or skill every month. Focus on taking strengths to a new level or improving weaknesses that are hindering performance. These actions should be documented and discussed regularly.

❷ **Communicate the company's strategic direction.** Make sure all employees know the company's strategic direction so that they understand how their performance and the performance of their teams support that direction. Make sure that they agree on their intended bottom-line results.

❸ **At the start of each year, set clear expectations.** Set objectives for each employee, with that employee's input, before the plan, fiscal, or performance year kicks off. Limit the objectives to six. These objectives should be large, overarching goals that can be measured using clearly articulated key performance indicators. When related to a sales goal, for instance, these indicators will be prospecting, obtaining appointments, closing the sale, and customer satisfaction.

❹ **Conduct minireviews monthly.** These reviews can be as simple as a chat over coffee, but they should cover progress toward objectives and development. Deliver any feedback with care, from the heart. Feedback on performance or skills carries an emotional charge. Feedback without feeling can destroy; skillful feedback with feeling is uplifting.

❺ **Conduct quarterly accountability reviews.** These reviews will assess whether any behaviors need to be changed or actions need to be taken to ensure that each employee's objectives and development plan are achieved. Leaders should be assessing progress and offering assistance in skill development if needed.

❻ **Conduct formal midyear evaluations.** Have a formal evaluation meeting to measure performance against objectives and the employee's development plan. The meeting will determine if any corrective actions are needed. Any new plan of action should be jointly agreed to and signed off on by the employee and supervisor.

❼ **Conduct final year-end appraisals.** Once again, employees' performance will be weighed against their objectives and development plan. This should not be difficult, because monthly, quarterly, and midyear reviews should provide everyone with a clear understanding of the relationship between work performance and expectations. This should not be a time for surprises. Conclude the meeting by setting objectives for the upcoming year.

In all of these appraisal reviews, it's best to list and prioritize what you want to discuss. Ensure that you are operating from the heart, with empathy, and that you are taking into account the feelings of the other person. Don't focus on the minor issues—they are easy to discuss, but if you start with them, you risk losing the employee's attention by the time you want to discuss major issues. Invite all employees shocked by their midyear or annual review to meet later to discuss the reasons for their astonishment.

If employees are shocked by the feedback they receive at any stage of the process, it is likely because they are not receiving regular feedback from their supervisor or leader. To avoid this, the company's leaders' merit pay system should be based on employee performance management benchmarks to ensure that performance management is a highly valued task that is taken seriously and done consistently. If leaders don't address performance, then employees cannot be held accountable.

A leader's role is to develop her people to their optimum potential. A big part of this is confronting reality and not being afraid to engage it. That means confronting underperformers. Everyone likes to be part of a winning team, and keeping poor performers as part of yours affects everybody's morale, motivation, and attitude. If you tolerate a low standard from underperformers, you'll create an environment in which people in the average performance zone will not feel any pressure to improve. You cannot afford to carry passengers.

You will know intuitively when a performance situation needs to be addressed. Right then—immediately—is the time to have the courageous conversation. Do not put this off. Do not put your head in the sand and hope the problem will go away. Taking quick, decisive action will give the underperformer the best chance of getting

DIAGNOSIS: EFFICIENT, BUT NOT EFFECTIVE

Watch for the employee who is very efficient, but not effective. The two traits may sound the same, but conflating them is similar to confusing activity with productivity. We all know people who are always busy, but whose productivity does not meet the required standards. The true achievers have learned that being efficient is necessary, but it is far more important to be effective. For example, the efficient leader is always on top of email and administrative items, responding in minutes, but can't find time to be with her team. The effective leader is out and about with his team and has set times to check email and to attend to administrative things.

Here are a few tips for focusing your team members on effectiveness:

- Know who your efficient workers are and who your effective workers are and address the issue during monthly minireviews.

- Educate people on the difference between the two traits and the importance of being effective.

- Have people create to-do lists in rank order, and then ask them if they put the easy tasks at the top or the important tasks at the top.

- At team meetings, have one of your effective people talk about how she works.

- Model effective behavior; don't shy away from important but daunting tasks.

- Address poor performance immediately and directly.

back on track, and it will ensure that you retain the respect of your other people, who are working hard to achieve the desired results. Acting promptly is a necessity for your well-being and the employee's. Too many leaders shy away from confrontation, and it becomes harder and harder to address the issue effectively as time goes by. If you let a problem fester, it will affect the whole team; they know about poor performers, usually before you do, and they wonder why they have to carry the extra workload. Conversely, when you address these performance issues, you will be respected as a strong leader.

Consistently, consistently, consistently address performance problems. They will not go away by themselves. At first it will take a lot of effort to continually address poor performers, but once you establish that you will quickly address any dip below set standards, employees will understand that inferior work will not be tolerated, and they will make sure to toe the line. If nonperformance is prevalent within a particular team, you have to look very closely at the

Lab Work

According to the State of Performance Management Study conducted by WorldatWork and Sibson Consulting, only 5 percent of organizations responding to the survey have effective performance management systems. The leading cause for this is that 71 percent of survey respondents lack the courage to discuss performance problems with employees. The other two reasons respondents point to are the belief that performance management is an HR issue (45 percent), and poor goal-setting habits (36 percent) ("Performance Management," *HR Focus*, 2007).

leader of that team. What example is he setting, and how consistently is he addressing performance issues?

Authentic leaders need also to be fierce competitors focused on winning and achieving, just like the leaders they compete against. The difference is that authentic leaders are operating in the feeling realm. Having empathy and compassion, particularly when dealing with difficult issues, goes a long way toward building trust and respect.

 I wouldn't have accepted the criticism from anyone, but *he was my line manager. He was the one who knew me best. And he had in mind good things for me.*
—FROM RODD WAGNER AND JAMES HARTER'S
12: THE ELEMENTS OF GREAT MANAGING

ANALYZE PERFORMANCE DEVIATION

So you know you need to confront performance issues as soon as you see them. If in the initial meeting with an underperformer you uncover issues that are affecting her results, you need to analyze these issues to determine how to proceed. The following performance deviation model will enable you to analyze these concerns and put you in a position to address them with a clear plan.

Performance Deviation Model

This model will help you determine if the source of the poor performance or performance deviation is a problem with skills or attitude. If the problem is in the employee's skills, provide "upskilling" through training, and if it is with attitude, get to the core issue and remove obstacles or provide an attitude tune-up (see Prescription 2). An attitude tune-up will entail really getting to know your employee, discovering what motivates him, digging deep to find the causes of his negative attitude, and then removing those obstacles if possible.

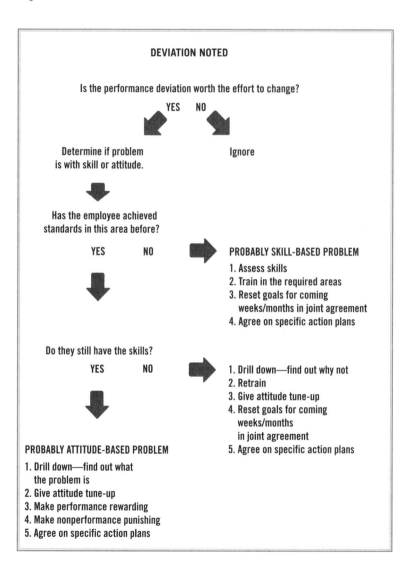

DEVIATION NOTED

Is the performance deviation worth the effort to change?

YES   NO

Determine if problem   Ignore
is with skill or attitude.

Has the employee achieved
standards in this area before?

YES   NO   **PROBABLY SKILL-BASED PROBLEM**
                           1. Assess skills
                           2. Train in the required areas
                           3. Reset goals for coming
                              weeks/months in joint agreement
                           4. Agree on specific action plans

Do they still have the skills?

YES   NO   1. Drill down—find out why not
                           2. Retrain
                           3. Give attitude tune-up
                           4. Reset goals for coming
                              weeks/months
                              in joint agreement
PROBABLY ATTITUDE-BASED PROBLEM   5. Agree on specific action plans

1. Drill down—find out what
   the problem is
2. Give attitude tune-up
3. Make performance rewarding
4. Make nonperformance punishing
5. Agree on specific action plans

EXAMPLES OF PERFORMANCE DEVIATIONS

Julie, who works alone as an administrator, has a young family and has been arriving up to fifteen minutes late on occasion. She is excellent at her job and does not leave until required tasks are completed.

Is performance deviation worth the effort to change? No, ignore it.

If Julie was working in a team and her late arrival was affecting others or others saw this as special treatment, then action would be required. This action could entail changing her hours to give her flexibility or a later start time.

Bill is a salesperson who had consistently met goals until two months ago; now he is achieving only around 80 percent of his target.

Is performance deviation worth the effort to change? Yes.

Has Bill previously achieved the standard in this area? Yes.

Does he still have the skills? Yes.

Have a coffee chat with Bill and get to the bottom of his changed performance. Drill down to ascertain if the changes are due to his attitude, and if so, find out what the causes are. If his difficulties are related to the business environment, agree to clear any obstacles if his reasoning is sound, or explain to him why changes cannot be made. Really listening to his concerns will help even if the perceived obstacles cannot be removed. If the problem is related to a personal issue and Bill is willing to freely talk about it, then you may be able to help by restructuring his working hours or role. Either way, really listening to Bill in a caring, authentic way will help.

Andrew has been with the company four months and is working on the customer service hotline. In the past week you have had two customers call back, explaining to others that Andrew had confused them. Prior to this, feedback from customers had been great.

Is performance deviation worth the effort to change? Yes.

Has standard been previously achieved in this area? Yes.

Does he still have the skills? Unknown.

As Andrew is so new in his role, it's best to drill down and find out if the problem is skill based or attitude based.

After meeting with Andrew you find he loves the role and has an excellent attitude. You discover that his supervisor neglected to send him to last week's training session on a new product release. Arrange a makeup session and meet with Andrew's supervisor to ensure that records are in place so training sessions are not overlooked in the future.

Pipeline Analysis

For employees who seem to be having a problem with skills, the next tool to use after the performance deviation model is the pipeline analysis. A leader who is managing employees who have a multistage process for completing their work, such as salespeople, should analyze the entire sales process to determine where the person's skills are leading to underperformance. For instance, if a salesperson isn't closing enough sales, is the problem in the initial contact, in obtaining appointments, at the appointment, in the follow-up, or in the closing technique? By looking at how many people the salesperson is contacting, how many potential clients are open to follow-up, and how many sales are being closed after follow-up, a manager will understand better what specific skills are lacking. By conducting this type of analysis, it will be clearly evident which area you need to focus on in the employee's plan for improvement.

Addressing Performance Deviation

When the deviation is considered substantial enough to take action, follow these five steps:

❶ **Clearly identify the deviation:** Write out the specific details of the problem before talking with the employee. Describe clearly to yourself why the behavior is a concern so you can articulate to the employee why this matter needs attention.

❷ **Explain:** Schedule a brief meeting with the employee to discuss the issue. Do not take the employee by surprise or interrupt him in the middle of a task. Set a time that is convenient. Be prepared, calm, and unemotional. Explain to the employee the cause of your concern and the reason why it needs to be addressed. Give him feedback on his good points and assure him that the exercise is aimed at getting his results back on track and that you are very confident he can attain the desired levels.

It is important to let the employee explain what might be causing the problem. You may see a different side to the situation, and everyone feels better after a fair hearing.

❸ **Find solutions:** Have the employee come up with solutions that will address the concern. Ensure that these steps will achieve the desired result. If the employee's suggestions are not suitable, you should modify or propose a solution. The employee must accept the responsibility to fix the issue. Advise him what you propose to do to assist, and ask if he feels there is anything else that you can do to help.

❹ Clarify: Reiterate the problem to the employee, and then confirm your commitment to help the employee get back on track. Ensure that the employee understands the solution. Put the objectives for improvement in writing, with proposed actions from both the employee and yourself. Both of you should sign the document to demonstrate your commitment and to help avoid any future misunderstandings.

❺ Follow up: Follow up with the employee by scheduling weekly action plan meetings, encouraging him if he is on plan, and looking at alternatives if the objectives are not being met. Stay on top of the situation until you are positive that your concerns have been resolved.

And remember: Keep a record of every interaction in writing. If the only option becomes terminating your underperforming team member, solid evidence will protect you and your organization.

COACH YOUR EMPLOYEES TO BETTER PERFORMANCE

A winning coach does not have a losing team. Employee nonperformance is often a result of managerial nonperformance. If you want your team members to be top performers, you need to lead them to that goal. True leaders will explore every avenue to bring nonperformers back on track.

A good leader is continually coaching and supporting her employees. Your people need to know that you are paying attention to what they do and how they are doing it. General coaching does not have to be a structured session; it is more powerful to make it a routine part of the way you interact with your people. If you are regularly seen providing spontaneous feedback when the need arises, corrective coaching sessions will run more smoothly and employees will be open to your suggestions because you have developed trusting and respectful relationships. This will flow into the whole workplace environment.

Corrective coaching, however, should be more structured than the coaching you do every day for all of your employees. An employee slated for corrective coaching may have emotions running high, so it is imperative that the leader displays a genuine desire to help in a caring and sincere way. Focus on the issues or performance concerns, not on the person, and display empathy and respect. Operate from the heart, be aware of the employee's feelings, and involve the employee in finding solutions. Making all the decisions yourself and simply telling an employee what will happen significantly lowers the chances of a successful outcome. As you create a program for an employee, keep in mind the following:

- Your own performance will speak louder than any of your words regarding standards of performance.

- Make sure to explain to your employee that the standard he is being measured against is the minimum standard set and agreed to by the entire team.

- Tailor the development program to the individual, keeping in mind his specific issues and linking the program to his known motivators when possible.

- Always look for improvement, constantly develop people, and be excited about their achievements.

- Provide all the tools needed for success; involve your employees in coming up with their own tools for success.

- Work with them to develop their skills and attitude, but be ready to take action if they do not improve and sustain that improvement.

- Keep an open mind to all the pertinent issues, and have compassion and empathy. Do not confuse empathy with sympathy, which is taking pity on the poor performer.

You must either modify your dreams or magnify your skills.
—JIM ROHN, AUTHOR AND MOTIVATIONAL SPEAKER

Shadowing or Joint Fieldwork

Shadowing an employee can be an incredibly informative way to assess their skills and offer useful feedback. The process can be a bit unnerving for employees, though, so it is the leader's responsibility to put them at ease by explaining the process and praising everything done well. Shadowing is even less intimidating if it is done on a regular basis for all employees. If you have leaders reporting to you, you might consider requiring them to shadow each of their employees once a quarter.

The shadowing process will be more productive if you have a standardized shadowing or joint fieldwork form that all leaders use. You can list the drivers of your business on this form for leaders to check for as they observe. If you're only shadowing your own team, you can create your own form with your drivers to ensure that you watch for the same practices with all employees. This will enable you to capture important information and offer effective and helpful

SHADOWING FORM

Name of Salesperson:	**Date:**
Name of Customer:	**Location:**

Customer Details:

SALES PROCESS

1. Building Rapport

What was done well?

What would you do differently?

Coach comments:

2. Identified Needs

What was done well?

What would you do differently?

Coach comments:

3. Recommend Solution

What was done well?

What would you do differently?

Coach comments:

4. Asked for the Business

What was done well?

What would you do differently?

Coach comments:

5. Did You Get the Business?

What was purchased—was it a win/win?

Would you have done anything differently?

Coach comments:

GENERAL COMMENTS

Manager

feedback to the employee at the end of the process. I've shown a basic form on the previous page, developed for a salesperson shadow.

If a coach is shadowing an employee while she is meeting with a client, he should not be taking notes on a form. He should wait until after the meeting is completed and write up his comments then. Immediately after the interview, while the experience is fresh in their minds, the coach and employee should each record their thoughts and observations and discuss. In the feedback session, a leader should use questions and phrases like the following:

- What do you think went very well in this interview?
- I was very impressed when you . . .
- I liked the way you positioned . . .
- Given the opportunity to redo this task/meeting/etc., is there anything you would change?

Once the coach has heard what the employee has to say about her own performance, the coach should share his observations and recommendations for how to improve. During this stage, it is important to be considerate of the employee's feelings and make sure that all feedback is constructive.

Skills Workshops

Skills workshops can be very helpful for underperformers, average performers, or even excellent performers who have certain weaknesses. Conduct these regularly, concentrating on the basic skills necessary within your team and aligning the content with your key business drivers. Focus on performance issues that seem to plague many of your team members.

Make these sessions compulsory for all employees who've been with your team for fewer than six months and all employees who are underachieving. You can also run advanced skills workshops that will be more helpful for your high achievers.

Structure your meeting content around the habits and skills of your top performers. Have these top people as presenters. Having them focus on an attribute or skill in which they excel can give other employees tips on how to improve their performances.

Have your employees use an action accelerator form (shown here) after skills workshops or meetings where ideas and initiatives are shared. Too often people leave these sessions intending to implement a number of changes, but without a specific commitment and plan for implementation, these changes rarely occur.

ACTION ACCELERATOR FORM

What are the three biggest insights for your business/performance from today's workshop?

1
2
3

What are the five actions you will implement?

ACTION	BY WHEN?
1	
2	
3	
4	
5	

THE TOUGH DECISION

If you've offered an underperforming employee all the appropriate development and training programs and you are confident, in your heart, that you have given him every opportunity to achieve success and he hasn't made the necessary changes, it is time to take tough action.

Remember that if we take more time in the recruitment and selection phase, have a committed employee development program, and work at keeping high morale and motivation in the work environment, the need to dismiss poor performers will be drastically reduced.

The need to dismiss an underachiever rarely occurs in an environment where the standards have been agreed on by all and a leader is authentically doing her utmost to develop her people to their optimum potential. In this type of team, consistent underachievers feel the pressure from the group and usually make their own decision to change or to move on.

When the time arises to remove a passenger, you will know, as will the employee and your team, that the decision you made was clearly the correct one.

YOUR NEW HEALTH REGIMEN

Set high expectations; never accept 80 percent effort or results.

Develop minimum standards with input from your team.

Model the level of performance you expect from others.

Develop a thorough performance appraisal process focused on providing regular and consistent feedback.

Clearly identify performance problems, promptly confront the issue, calmly address it with the employee, brainstorm solutions with him, and confirm his commitment to change.

Use the performance deviation model to determine if inferior performance is a problem with skills or attitude so you know how to help solve the problem.

Coach employees to the level of performance you expect.

Be prepared to terminate employees who can't be rehabilitated.

PRESCRIPTION 5

THE CURE FOR EMPLOYEES WHO AREN'T
CONNECTING WITH CUSTOMERS

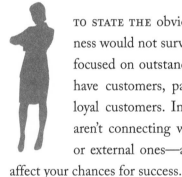 TO STATE THE obvious, without customers, your business would not survive. But without employees who are focused on outstanding customer service, you wouldn't have customers, particularly the most valuable kind: loyal customers. In any organization, employees who aren't connecting with customers—internal customers or external ones—are a weak link that will negatively affect your chances for success.

Leaders of the most successful organizations understand the importance of getting and keeping employees focused on offering great customer service. It's the employees and the companies who set high expectations for service and then meet or even exceed those expectations who come out on top. If you have employees who can't seem to connect with customers or who don't understand the importance of exceptional customer service, you need to address the issue immediately.

Lab Work

According to the Walker Loyalty Report conducted by Walker Information, a company that has been researching the customer experience for the last sixty-five years, four in every ten customers are willing to pay a little more for retail products in exchange for a qualified sales assistant. This gives us an indication of the value that customers place on receiving good customer care (Laposky, 2004).

When we really look at developing people and their skills (which is the single most important activity of any leader, in case you haven't gotten that point yet) we need to be clear on what we want to achieve. What drives everything we do? Call it results or call it growth, it's what we all know can be produced and sustained only through superior customer service.

This is why the fifth prescription I offer is:

R_X If you want your employees to connect with customers and deliver exceptional service, you have to create a culture of valuing customers, make sure everybody understands how to wow your customers, develop exceptional customer service skills in your people, and measure customer connection regularly.

CREATE A CULTURE OF VALUING CUSTOMERS

As with anything a leader wants to focus on, he has to lead the way, showing belief, passion, and an excellent attitude. This is particularly important in customer service because it is easy for employees to slip into the "what-a-pain-in-the-ass" mentality, even employees with otherwise good attitudes. To keep your employees upbeat and positive about customer relationship building and care, you have to make sure your entire culture supports that focus and attitude. Any organization where the customer is not the top priority has lost its way and needs to quickly refocus.

The first step in building a culture of valuing customers, then, is examining your vision of customer care—what you really believe in your heart about how your customer should feel. If you are fuzzy on this point, your people will be too. It is imperative for all leaders in an organization to constantly display a passion for achieving outstanding service. Employees need to see and experience through words and actions an ongoing belief that the customer is number one. To achieve this type of culture, there are a few key organizational elements to explore.

Systems and Processes

In any organization, there are internal and external systems that affect a customer's experience and the abilities of employees to deliver great experiences. Make sure that there aren't any processes that inhibit the delivery of great customer service: for example, brutally complex approval processes, databases that aren't useful or user-friendly, or outdated communication systems. Continually work to simplify systems your customer comes into direct contact

with and obtain ideas regularly from your frontline staff to facili-
tate this process. Look at each system from a customer perspective:
"What would my customer say about this?" If she would not say,
"Wow, this gives brilliant service!" you have work to do.

Initiative Culture

Enable your people to provide immediate and generous responses
to customer issues. Empower them to fix problems on the spot, up
to a certain dollar amount based on their experience and expertise.
The dollar limit you assign will vary depending on the type of your
business, but keep in mind the long-term value of a delighted customer. Often it is not the amount of money spent fixing a problem
but the expediency of the solution and the trust in staff it shows
that impress the customer.

Highlight Memorable Service

Ensure that all aspects of your culture support great customer care.
Create reward systems that take into account what you are trying
to achieve in this area. For example, Wachovia's reward principles
emphasize the importance of resolving customer concerns and providing sound financial advice. They secure accountability by asking
all frontline staff to hand out Gallup customer surveys for customers
to use to confidentially evaluate their effectiveness.

At team meetings highlight employees who provide outstanding service and share customer testimonials. Have awards for customer service excellence, not only for frontline staff but also for
other internal areas seemingly out of direct contact. Keep customer care at the forefront of everyone's mind and explain how all

departments need to pull together to achieve outstanding service. Make sure that you reward great service to internal as well as external customers.

Have Fun

Create fun activities with a "service" theme for staff. One method I have used successfully is to create teams and have them search for the holy grail of elusive great service moments. They present their findings at a team meeting where everyone votes on the winners. Also, have fun with customers. Build relationships with them based on a win-win philosophy. The benefits of instilling a fun atmosphere in your organization and with your customers are many.

- Customer loyalty increases, leading to more future sales.
- You create customer advocates, who provide warm referrals.
- Recruiting great people is easier as you become known as an employer of choice.
- Interaction among coworkers improves.
- Morale improves as positive customer responses keep everyone in a better mood.
- There are fewer employee issues with tardiness or absenteeism.
- Employees' lives are enriched at work, and they stay with you.
- You earn a positive company reputation.
- Discounting products or services will not be necessary, as customers truly perceive an increased value in superior service.
- It enhances your bottom line.

EXPLORE YOUR WOW FACTORS

Let's acknowledge some important realities of conducting business today. Marketing has become inescapable, competition in most industries is fierce, and most customers face many demands on their time and attention. The challenges here are apparent: It can be tougher than ever before to reach customers.

However, wherever there is a challenge, I see an opportunity for excellence to shine through. One piece of incredibly good news in all this is that truly exceptional customer care has a greater impact than ever before, because so few individuals and companies deliver it. Today, when a salesperson does connect with a customer, it's more critical and more beneficial than ever to wow that customer, potentially creating an advocate for your business and a source of referrals—which is the best, most successful marketing of all.

In workshops on this topic, I begin by asking people to recall a significant retail purchase they've made in the last few years that was marked by truly exceptional customer service; the type of service that has you wanting to tell one and all about your experience. It is a sad reflection on the state of service that most everyone can recall a customer service horror story, but it is rare that someone can recount a time when he received absolutely sensational service. Can you recall such an experience of outstanding service that had you referring family and friends to the business? Reflection on this can help you visualize the very real opportunity available to you when you can wow customers, and it helps you form your own definition of what the elusive wow factor means when it comes to your products and services.

> A moment of truth is anytime a customer comes into contact with anyone in our organization in a way that they can get an impression. How do we answer the phone? How do we check people in? How do we greet them on our planes? How do we interact with them during flights? How do we handle baggage claim? What happens when a problem occurs?
>
> —JAN CARLZON, FORMER PRESIDENT OF
> SCANDINAVIAN AIRLINES SYSTEMS

To highlight the importance of delivering a wow experience and the many different ways that can be done, I'll share three stories with you. These stories help differentiate excellent service from service that delivers a true wow factor. The first incident I'll share occurred in the late 1990s. When shopping for a stereo system in Sydney, Australia, I encountered a brilliant salesperson. Allan went out of his way to explain systems and options in language I understood, and after he had really listened to my needs, I was delighted, but surprised, to hear him tell me not to purchase the model I was interested in. He advised me that there was another model due to arrive within fourteen days that was smaller and easier to operate, yet the sound was at least as good, and the pricing was similar.

I received a call when the stereo arrived and an excellent tutorial on how to install and get the most out of the system. Two days after the purchase I received another call from Allan; this time he was checking to see if the installation went smoothly and if I had any questions.

Allan's approach was authentic, and not overbearing. He made the effort to come down to my level when explaining technical aspects of the system; the whole process was about me and my needs. His goal was clearly to ensure that I was comfortable with the system's features and able to use its full capabilities to enhance my enjoyment. I was so impressed by this experience—demonstrating excellent service but nothing extraordinary—that, upon learning Allan had a finance-related degree, I recruited him as a financial planner.

For a more remarkable customer care story, I'll retell the experience of a friend I'll call Dale, who purchased a Lexus in Australia. During the initial test-drive, his salesperson, Jeffrey, called attention to the excellent stereo system and its features, such as a nine-speaker array, programming capabilities, and automatic muting when the car phone rings. He casually asked my friend about his favorite music and learned that Dale was a Rod Stewart fan.

Several months later, after testing numerous vehicles, Dale decided on the Lexus he had driven with Jeffrey. Imagine his surprise when, upon receiving the car, he turned on the stereo system and it began playing a Rod Stewart greatest hits CD!

Jeffrey had applied subtlety and surprise to great effect, creating a "magic moment" for his customer that resulted in Dale telling family, friends, and associates the story. Dale was pleased with the car, but the wow factor was in the CD story. Although it hadn't cost Jeffrey much in terms of time or expense, his extra effort had the potential to create tremendous goodwill toward him and his dealership, as well as referrals for potential future sales.

For the final story, I'll turn to Lexus's parent company, Toyota. Toyota announced in 1987 that it was creating Lexus, a new division devoted to building the best luxury vehicles in the world. The cars sold very well, but only months into the venture, the one thing that Lexus feared happened. The company learned of two cars having problems, an issue with the cruise control. Lexus faced a decision: It could quietly fix these cars and wait to see if others surfaced, or it could issue a recall and let the world know that Lexus engineering was not perfect.

As Lexus was counting on its dealers to deliver service far beyond that of other automotive brands, it decided to set an example, one that is still talked about in the automotive industry to this day. Lexus recalled every LS400 it had sold. But the real story lies in how they did it. Every recall notice included a letter of apology from the company and a promise that, if needed, the dealer would pick up the vehicle and deliver it back when finished. On top of that, customers were advised that when the issue had been repaired, their cars would be detailed inside and out and returned to them with a full tank of gas.

Insiders say that this recall marked the day that Lexus proved that what made a brand a luxury brand was its customer focus. Since that time Lexus has consistently won automotive industry luxury awards, and it has achieved this with a commitment to excellence in customer service that it will not compromise.

THESE STORIES REALLY illustrate how to aim beyond very good or even excellent service. They highlight several important qualities to consider when aiming for your own wow factor.

- Deliver a totally unexpected extra touch that is significant enough to command attention and make the customer want to tell others.

- Don't ask customers to pay for the extra touch; deliver superb moments even after the sale has been completed.

- Make sure that the wow factor is personalized to the needs and interests of the customer. It shows the salesperson's personal attentiveness and real care for the customer. You may have some standard solutions in place that employees can turn to, but teach them to be flexible and creative.

- Make the moment subtle and respectful, taking the gesture beyond a stunt aimed at getting business.

- "Double-wow" loyal longtime customers even when you know they are not going to seek your services elsewhere. They will continue to be your advocates but with more exuberance.

To better understand the nature of the wow moment, consider whether Jeffrey at the Lexus dealership would have generated the same impact with a different type of gesture and different timing. He might have learned that Dale enjoyed Starbucks cappuccino, for example, and sent a text message to have one waiting in the show-room after the test-drive. A pleasant surprise, certainly, and Dale would have thanked him, but he would have known that the gesture was directed at getting the sale.

To keep your employees focused on these types of wow moments, try the following:

- Brainstorm with employees possible ways of creating magical moments for customers.

- Find out if your staff is impressing your customers, and how. If they are, share your research with your employees to let them know what's working. If they aren't, find out why, and focus everybody's attention on fixing it.

- Post wow factor stories in a common area for employees to read. This will help inspire them and give them some ideas on how they can wow their customers.

- Research outstanding examples of service constantly as you go about your daily life. It is amazing how infrequently we encounter someone prepared to go the extra mile to satisfy us. When you find someone who is, send employees to experience what superior customer service is all about—especially send the ones in need of an attitude adjustment!

■ Implement, inspect, measure, recognize, and reward the delivery of truly memorable, outstanding customer care throughout your company.

Remember, don't settle for average—strive for excellence and wow.

 If you want to create raving fans, you don't just announce *it. You have to plan for it—you have to visualize it. What kind of experience do you want your customers to have as they interact with every aspect of your organization?*

—KEN BLANCHARD, "BLANCHARD'S DREAM," FROM *CUSTOMER MANIA,* COAUTHORED WITH JIM BALLARD AND FRED FINCH

Make Sure Your Products Are Wowing Customers

Your customers need to know and understand what it is that makes your company special. You as a leader need to analyze your product offerings from the eyes of your customers while comparing your products/services against those of your competitors. You may offer the best guarantee in the business, your warranty may exceed those of your competitors, your product may be all natural or chemical free, your payment options and interest rates may be superior. Emphasize whatever it is that sets your product off from others like it.

When you find your competitive advantages, they can be your product wow factors and the things you advertise, the strengths that your competitors may not have. Then you need to look at your product offerings regularly and match them to customer feedback to see if they are really what the customer wants. Hiring a contractor to professionally obtain your customers' feedback on a consistent basis is money well spent.

But, when you obtain this customer feedback, listen, and act on what it tells you! You need to be especially careful with products that you see as your signature offerings. The following story from Starbucks explains what I mean.

According to Sydney Finkelstein's book *Why Smart Executives Fail,* Starbucks created a generation of coffee snobs, but this snobbery created a blind spot early on among the company's top executives. When they found out that weight-conscious customers wanted skim milk for their lattes, the execs were appalled. They were convinced that the consumer needed a quality coffee drink, while the customers (those folks with the money) wanted something that maybe didn't taste as good, but was easier on their waistline. This is a classic case, but not an unusual one, of executives living out their product dream despite what the customer is crying out for. Finally sanity prevailed, and now we can order skinny lattes while Starbucks still makes a fortune. Recently I have noticed that Starbucks has gone a step further, now offering 2 percent milk for the middle-ground people (like me) who want a healthier alternative without compromising taste.

Use Your Wow Factor to Build Relationships

The constant pursuit of the wow factor does not apply solely to business you haven't yet secured. In all relationships, it's vital to keep injecting energy and surprise so that neither party takes the other's effort entirely for granted.

A great illustration of the fact that you can still wow a long-time customer comes from my banking years, when we retained an event-planning company to handle our sales conferences and events for top performers. Although this firm did an excellent job through the years, providing great incentive ideas and execution as well as the typical planning tasks, periodically we would question the real value of their services internally. My staff went so far as to suggest we take over managing the events to save the 15 percent cost the planning company charged per event. It was a suggestion I began to seriously consider.

During one conference, we had scheduled an especially exciting event, an excursion for eighty high achievers to a tall bluff on beautiful Fraser Island in Queensland, Australia, overlooking the ocean at sunset. I had decided not to provide refreshments on this particular outing, but I was having second thoughts. I could justify the decision to myself in a number of ways, but in truth, I was feeling like I had cut an unnecessary corner. But the principal of the event-planning company, Jack, took great care to solve an issue I hadn't even told him about. On the short walk to the bluff, we all heard a rustle in the bush and out stepped servers in black tie, with hors d'oeuvres and champagne! I was impressed. Then, as we all stood on the bluff admiring the sunset, we heard live music from a string quartet that had also been hidden. Jack leaned over and whispered, "No worries. This is on me."

Whether Jack had any specific sense that our commitment to his company sometimes wavered I can't say for certain. What is certain is that the extras stood out. Jack and his team really took a well-executed event over the top, into the realm of the exceptional and never-to-be-forgotten. I appreciated Jack's not taking us for granted, going the extra mile, and valuing us as a customer to the extent that simply delivering expected service wasn't enough. I knew we had the right company in charge of our event planning; never again during my tenure did we consider taking the business in-house. And, of course, I've told many people this story as an example of outstanding customer care and excellent relationship building, which has surely helped Jack's business.

DEVELOP EXCEPTIONAL CUSTOMER SERVICE SKILLS IN YOUR TEAM

In the many award ceremonies I've attended for top performers of one type or another, I've heard moving speeches acknowledging the support of leadership, the inspiration of team collaboration, and the

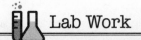

Lab Work

A Walker Loyalty Report conducted in 2005 for the communications industry found a significant correlation between customer loyalty and company financial performance, which echoed findings from past studies of other industries. The report found that companies that scored high marks in developing and maintaining customer loyalty experienced an average of 20 percent more revenue growth than those companies with lagging customer loyalty scores. Loyalty leaders' average operating margin was 22 percent higher over three years, and their stock prices were 34 percent higher over five years when compared to customer loyalty laggards (Marr, 2005).

importance of positive morale and company culture. But another, more striking common element in these speeches has been the heart and passion in these top performers' words about their customers. These people bared their souls talking about the satisfaction they receive when they exceed customer expectations.

This level of personal fulfillment is the reward that awaits people you can successfully lead along the path to unfailingly putting customers first, and never settling for less than the exceptional when it comes to service. It's up to you to do more than preach the gospel and set the strategy, however. Ongoing training will be indispensable in achieving the outstanding results you demand. Unifying your organization around the absolute value of wowing the customer is essential, and as with all other principles we discuss, you must remember that the strategy is only as good as your discipline and rigor in implementing it.

Superior customer service is the key to superb results, but unfortunately, you will have players on your team who need to be convinced that is the case. These people are missing the link between the two, and they are also not seeing that providing outstanding service will enrich their jobs and make coming to work more enjoyable.

You need to train and empower these doubters to provide brilliant service. Much of the training falls to leaders, but you can use top performers to help with the process. Select the best to train the rest. To unconvinced employees, having their peers involved in training gives the training credibility. Ensure that the selected trainers are respected by their peers and truly are, in everyone's eyes, providing superior service.

There's another benefit of working on developing these skills, or any skills, in your employees. When you develop your people, you indirectly enhance your marketing and advertising campaigns. Fulfilled employees feel valued and are more likely to be engaged, and they will pass that motivation and passion for work on to their customers. They will be advocates for your company, just as you want your customers to be advocates for your company.

> 🙶   *For my customer, I may not have the answer,*   🙸
> *but I'll find it. I may not have the time, but I'll make it.*
> —UNKNOWN

A Company That Wows

Chip and Amy run Auto Craftsmen, an auto repair business in Montpelier, Vermont. They provide an excellent example of how to build a business through superior customer service—wowing your customer.

Currently they have three technicians (not called "mechanics," as these days in auto repairs the work is predominately computer based and technical), as well as Marc, who is the service adviser, Chip as foreman, and Amy looking after marketing, financials, and community education.

Chip, who is a fabulous technician, started the business in 1980 and ran it very successfully as a one-man show. Amy joined the business in 1995 and spent her first eight years as service adviser. During this time she was an avid learner, watching repairs and studying tech magazines. She wanted to really learn the business to ensure that her conversations with customers about their problems were meaningful. Plus, as the service adviser, she was first contact for most customers.

In 2001 Chip and Amy purchased new equipment, expanded the premises, and hired more technicians. All they needed were more customers! Amy hired Ron Ipac from Cinron Marketing, who had built a business teaching auto repair shops how to grow their businesses. Many of Chip and Amy's marketing ideas came from this coaching relationship. They still work with Cinron and are now part of the Pinnacle Group, an association of eighty independent auto repair shops that receive specialized advice from Ron and have regular group meetings to share ideas and initiatives.

When you call Auto Craftsmen, Marc answers, and you are immediately impressed with the friendly and informative responses to your questions. Then, upon entering, you immediately realize that this is not your average auto repair shop. The waiting room looks fabulous, clean, and comfortable. Classical music is playing, and you are given the Auto Craftsmen difference book to browse as you wait for Chip to meet you for your no-obligation initial appointment.

If you haven't been wowed yet, the interview with Chip will do it! Chip's knowledge of vehicles is second to none, yet you do not feel overwhelmed as he takes you through the process at your speed, thoroughly educating you to help you make informed decisions. This builds trust right from the outset, and you feel empowered with your newfound knowledge of your vehicle and safe operating tips. A road test follows, during which Chip will explain the reasons he is testing things like steering, brakes, and acceleration.

When you return to the office, Chip provides written recommendations based on your specific circumstances, your vehicle's current condition, its anticipated annual mileage, and the amount of time you think you will retain the vehicle. You are given a folder to take home to review the recommendations and discuss them if there is another decision maker involved.

If you book the next appointment, after the work is completed you receive a follow-up call to ensure that all your problems were fixed. If not, you are invited back to have the issues rectified at no charge.

From the initial telephone call and the moment you step into the waiting room right through the entire process, the communication to customers is excellent. No wonder the majority of Auto Craftsmen's new customers are referrals from their raving advocates!

Chip and Amy aren't content to wow their customers and their community only from their shop, however. Their monthly newsletter, available electronically or in hard copy, has safety tips, recipes, jokes, and information on their specials, such as a free winterization check or a brakes special where brake pads and labor are free.

On a regular basis they have promotions aimed at giving back to the community: Toys for Tots and The Community Food Shelf are their two favorite charities. The promotions provide win/wins or "double wows": the customer receives a special discount for her contribution to a worthwhile cause, and the needy in the community benefit too.

Chip and Amy are passionate about educating their customers and the general community about their vehicles, especially for safety purposes. They also raise awareness of the knowledge and expertise a technician requires, and how hard he works to ensure that your vehicle is operating safely and efficiently. Amy provides education classes for schoolchildren and driver education classes, and she speaks to many groups on auto safety.

Amy's next goal is to launch a TV program, "Amy's Garage," that will take her passion for educating the public to a new level.

Chip and Amy are not only building a great business by wowing their customers, they are enriching the general community with their efforts to educate their community members, increase auto safety, and give back to the area.

Hire and Train Emotionally Intelligent Frontline Staff

Your recruiting guidelines for people who interact with customers should have a focus on emotional intelligence (EQ). EQ is the ability to perceive, assess, and manage one's own and others' feelings and emotions, to discriminate among them, and to use this information in thought and action. If you hire people who have high innate EQ, you will have a head start in connecting with your customers.

The reason emotional intelligence is so important is because emotionally charged moments, not humdrum ones, are when you have a chance to wow a customer and earn her loyalty. A customer's flight was canceled. A customer lost her traveler's checks. A customer needs the goods tomorrow. Different businesses trigger different emotional moments, but regardless of the situation, these are the times when a business has the opportunity to shine and differentiate itself.

I recall one of these times in my father's butcher shop. A regular customer came in and ordered a few items, all cheap cuts of meat. My father sensed something odd and asked, "Mrs. Jones, this is nothing like your regular weekly order. Has our meat been fine?"

"Oh yes, the meat has been great. It's the children; I've had two of them ill and that's very expensive, and this week I need to cut back on food."

"Well, that is not going to happen. You have been a loyal customer of mine for years, and your usual weekly order plus a bonus to help them heal is on me this week."

The words brought tears to her eyes, and she thanked him profusely. Within the next seven days my father had four new customers sent in by Mrs. Jones. It was that emotionally charged moment that turned a loyal customer into a raving advocate.

You need to hire people who can handle such moments with empathy and respect. It is imperative to focus on this kind of compassionate quick thinking during your training with both new and old employees. This training should focus on listening: really listening beyond the words and compassionately delving deeper to find the real reasons for certain customer behaviors. Teach your employees to be ready; don't let them miss these unique opportunities to excel and create a customer advocate!

Focus People on Exceeding Customer Expectations

Uncovering and acknowledging a customer's expectations is a fundamental sales skill, critical to building business and achieving excellent overall results. Going beyond the call of duty to exceed those expectations—religiously and consistently—is what makes winners and takes a business on to the next level of success. However, there is a fine line to walk in terms of expectations because of a simple rule of human perception and behavior: While exceeding expectations can delight a customer, not meeting expectations is a sure way to lose him. So, the best path to follow is to tell customers what they can expect, honestly; deliver on your promises; and then work to exceed customers' expectations whenever possible.

Of course, it's unwise to set customer expectations at a level that cannot be delivered. Your employees need to learn how to avoid making best-case promises when there is a likelihood they won't be kept. That is a certain recipe for canceled orders and lost customers. However, if you want to differentiate yourself in the market, you must set an expectation that your people will aim for the exceptional and the memorable in every customer encounter.

One lighter-hearted but very useful technique I suggest is what I call "the mother of all customer-service rules." For those struggling to understand or put in practice the principles of overdelivering and exceeding customer expectations, I recommend asking them to put "Mom" in front of their unaccommodating responses to customers, as in "Mom, I'm sorry, but that's not my responsibility." "Mom, the person you've asked to speak with is at lunch now, and I can't help you with your problem." "Mom, may I put you on hold while I deal with another call?" The simple questions *Would you say that to your mother? Would you treat her this way? Or would you try to determine a better solution?* can help people understand better the level of customer service they are expected to deliver. The approach can be very effective in emphasizing the importance of courtesy and care beyond the ordinary.

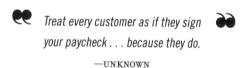

Treat every customer as if they sign
your paycheck . . . because they do.
—UNKNOWN

Don't Let Employees Disagree!

Of the many recommendations, rules, and practices you emphasize with your people relative to customer service, I believe one requires special attention. The opposite of exceeding a customer's expectations is to argue or disagree with that customer about the validity of those expectations. Arguing with a customer is the single biggest mistake you can make—and is potentially very damaging to your business.

Many studies demonstrate that a person will tell far more people about a negative service experience than she will tell about a positive one. In rough numbers, the word-of-mouth effect might break down as follows:

- A person who has a very good customer experience tells four people.

- A person who rates the experience as excellent may tell twelve people.

- Accounts of a poor experience are likely to reach twenty people.

- If you disagree or argue with a customer, that customer may tell *forty or more people*.

Nothing good comes from arguing or disagreeing with a customer. The warning it sends to other potential customers will be very powerful and have wide reach. Sharing this insight with your people is very important and powerful. Repeating it whenever necessary should be a priority for you as a leader, and for all your team members too.

When you reiterate the importance of not arguing with customers, though, it's also a great opportunity to remind your people that you can't please every customer, every time, and not everyone will be your customer. There are many ways to let customers know that unfortunately you won't be able to meet their expectations without angering them. However, this should happen only when it really is impossible to meet their expectations, never because an employee just doesn't feel like trying. Following are some tips to try:

- First restate your value proposition to justify a reasonable level of expectation. For instance, explain why the price is set where it is if your customer wants you to go lower than you can.

- Next, try to find another way to satisfy her needs. If you can't lower the price, maybe there's some other benefit you can offer, such as a period of free service.

- Then actually make an effort to see if an exception can be made in her case. For some customers and some situations, exceptions can be made.

- Finally, if reasonable compromise and your best effort(s) don't get results, it's time to part politely, without inflaming any bad will.

Teach your people how to value a customer's lifetime value. If a customer is going to spend $100 a week at your business and will live in the area for twenty-five years, they have a lifetime value of $130,000 ... In that case, it's certainly not worth fighting over a returned item for a few dollars, and very worthwhile to be innovative and find ways to wow him!

Lifetime value = annual $ x potential years as customer

Train for Persistence and Follow-Through

Another story may help you encourage the virtues of a "never give up" attitude, solid prospecting, and long-term management in your people as regards keeping in contact with prospective customers.

A very dedicated financial planner, let's call him William, had the opportunity to speak with a prospective client three years before the gentleman planned to retire. This prospect made it very clear he was checking around with various companies to evaluate investment options for his retirement payout, and the conversation ended amicably.

Over the next three years, William kept making scheduled contact with his long-term prospect, initially once every six months, then once per month as the planned retirement approached. When this man eventually retired, he visited William and invested his entire $2.5 million payout. The primary reason he gave? William was the one and only planner to keep in touch, despite promises from four others. This same client went on to refer numerous clients in similar situations, due to William's diligence and effort in following up *without applying pressure.*

Teach the Supreme Value of Referrals

Every business, every leader, and every employee on the ground level should aim for outstanding customer service—if for no other reason (and I've cited many) than to build results through referrals. What could be a bigger win or a bigger business driver than having customers sell your services for you to their family and friends?

The likelihood of you building a solid, expanding referral channel is directly linked to your success in consistently exceeding customer expectations. In many cases, this means providing requested assistance outside the norm. For example, I recall a situation when a customer entered our bank and asked for help in completing pension papers because he could not read or write English. One of our planners took the time and made the effort to fulfill the request. Then she took the extra step of forwarding these documents to the appropriate pension office and attaching a note with her contact information in case questions arose. Soon afterward, she began receiving direct referrals from many of this happy customer's non-English-speaking friends, and these referrals enabled her to generate significant new business.

It is an established fact that businesses that provide exceptional customer service and focus on obtaining referrals from their delighted customers will get at least 25 percent of their new customers by referral.

The absolute best opportunity to ask for referrals is whenever you receive a customer compliment. These opportunities should never be missed, because they can be seized subtly and engagingly, with no extra time investment. Remind your representatives frequently that if a customer says, for example, "You made this process so simple, and handled all of our concerns so well," they must respond appropriately.

The best response to a compliment is to say something like "I love receiving compliments. It really makes me feel great about the service we provide, and I've truly enjoyed doing business with you as well. The best compliment I ever receive, however, is to have you refer your family and friends to me, because that's how I build my business and continue to have such fulfilling encounters with people like you." Of course, it needs to sound authentic, so each employee might have a different approach.

The next step? Stop talking and wait for a response.

Teach Employees How to Earn Advocates by Being Advocates

Your commitments to delivering exceptional service and building a referral business should permeate all your encounters with customers. It has helped me to think in terms of a "progress chart" for customers, with key milestones:

Prospect: The first interaction with a prospective customer

Customer: The first time a prospect does business with you

Client: The second time the customer does business with you

ADVOCATE: WHEN A CLIENT PROVIDES YOU WITH VALUABLE REFERRALS

Gaining and nurturing advocates is one of the most important priorities of your sales organization. Creating win-win situations with these customers is very important, so always be on the lookout for opportunities to refer prospects to your customers' businesses. This means truly partnering with your loyal and trusted customers. It's also essential to be advocates for your customers in turn whenever they have a problem or concern. Simply stated, the role of anyone face-to-face with a customer is to understand and, if possible, adopt his perspective, empathize, and help him fight his battle. Often, even if the result is not everything the customer wanted, you will have earned a customer—or even an advocate—for life.

MEASURE CUSTOMER CONNECTION REGULARLY

Setting and enforcing an expectation of outstanding service is essential. In order to execute that strategy, it's equally important to establish disciplined measures of how the customer feels when dealing with your people. Too many businesses believe they know what their customers want without asking. Don't join the throng of businesses opening doors for competitors because they refuse to understand their customers, or worse, they hear what their customers want but fail to deliver. Ask what your customers want, listen, and take action. Constantly look at new ways of obtaining customer feedback. The table shown on page 149 describes some of the methods I've used to gain this valuable information.

Measurement and follow-through are critical for all these methods. As you can see, each can be useful and highly beneficial, and you may want to apply them all at times to get a clear picture of how your people are performing. Remember to focus on the number of

Method	Key Stipulations	Advantages	Limitations
Quarterly written customer surveys	Ensure questions are specific, relevant, objective, and measurable; encourage and leave room for written comments specific to the customer's experience.	Simple to implement and administer; allows respondents time to provide thoughtful feedback	Likely to get limited response; results can be difficult to interpret quickly and productively
Mystery shopping	Engage a professional company with this specialty; ensure realistic expectations by focusing on a maximum of five key drivers that can be objectively measured; aim to "shop" each representative at least three times to gain fair, accurate insight.	Best replication of actual customer interaction; can often provide clear, direct insight into areas that need improvement (or recognition/reward)	Requires significant cost investment to execute properly; may require extra justification to maintain trust with representatives being evaluated
Customer callbacks	All managers should be making these calls; callbacks should be made within ten days of the original customer interaction; unsuccessful contacts should be included. It is a good idea to have customer service staff and salespeople make these calls as well; it can really open their eyes to find out how a customer actually feels.	Provides an engaging, nonthreatening opportunity to reconnect with customers; challenging questions with direct business impact can be posed; feedback can be acted upon immediately with individual training or team development	Requires manager-level commitment and effort

"highly satisfied" customers in your surveys. In aiming for excellence in customer service, we need to achieve more than "satisfied customers."

My personal favorite among these three methods is conducting customer callbacks because of the advantages listed and the
high level of connection and adaptability for virtually any business.
I highly recommend instilling this disciplined practice among any
corps of managers, and frequently emphasizing its importance once
it is in place.

As a leader, you can also try "doing business with yourself" to
gain direct insight into your performance and customer connection
levels. It can be immensely valuable and enlightening to

- test the experience of calling in an order to your company;

- test calling in with a realistic customer problem or concern;
  and

- test other call-in scenarios reflecting all the various reasons
  customers contact your people.

A common objection to employing some of these measurement methods is that your people may feel over-monitored or
"spied upon." Your answer to this objection begins with the way
you introduce the practice and its purpose and must be carried
through every step, including how you act on the information you
acquire by developing your employees. Emphasize the following:

- The point of measuring performance is to develop people and
  improve overall performance.

- There is no substitute for a real-world measurement of satisfaction to determine whether your company is delivering exceptional customer service and care.

- The company and its management are making the time and
  cost investment necessary to succeed.

■ Low ratings will be approached, first and foremost, as development challenges and opportunities. Everyone—from top performers on through the ranks—is expected to aim for constant improvement.

The hard truth here is that those who object to having their performance measured typically have something to hide. The sooner you challenge such individuals to commit to improving, the sooner you can determine whether they have—or are willing to adopt—the attitude, intentions, and focus that success requires. This is yet another important benefit of measuring customer satisfaction.

Another way to measure feedback is to teach employees to listen, overhear remarks, be nosy, ask questions, read between the lines,

 Lab Work

The Valtera Corporation did a study comparing employee customer-focused engagement to customer satisfaction. Fifty firms were measured for satisfaction using the American Customer Satisfaction Index (ACSI), and then employee engagement was determined by having employees rate their customer connections. For example, employees might rate high or low on "We help customers beyond what is expected" or "It is the custom in this organization to help customers." The report found that companies scoring higher in customer-focused engagement also experienced better scores in customer satisfaction. This had a monetary impact as well: a one-point increase in an ACSI score boosted return on investment by an average of 11.4 percent (Schneider, 2006).

and find out what their customers really think. Start a program in which all staff have the opportunity to call customers to obtain feedback. This is an excellent training tool when used correctly.

When you increase your engagement with customers, their satisfaction rises, and so does your revenue!

PURE INSPIRATION: THE WEDDING STORY

I've saved one very compelling story for last in this prescription. I've told this story many times, and you may find the retelling meaningful for your people to emphasize what can come from going the extra mile to please a customer.

A German man contacted a financial planner, let's call her Diane, at my bank to discuss the possibility of Australian investments. The meeting went very well, resulting in a $500,000 investment. Several weeks later, Diane received a call from this same client, now back in Germany. He told her he wanted to get married the next month. She first laughed and remarked on the suddenness of the proposal. The German gentleman quickly clarified that he and his intended bride wanted to have their wedding in Sydney around Christmastime. The man asked Diane if she could arrange a marriage celebrant, find a place for the ceremony overlooking the harbor, and book a quiet restaurant with a harbor view for lunch for eight people.

What a request! Diane told her client she would make the effort and get back to him, marveling at the improbability of fulfilling all aspects of this request. Her first success was when she phoned the prospective marriage celebrant. Not only did the woman agree to perform the ceremony, her husband also remarked, "If you're treating customers this well, I'm going to look into bringing my investments back to your bank." It had turned out that the celebrant and her husband were former customers of this particular bank and branch.

Diane was also successful booking a space for the wedding in the beautiful Sydney Botanical Gardens, overlooking the spectacular Sydney Opera House and the harbor. But, as she had feared, it appeared impossible to book a quiet, appropriate restaurant with a few weeks' notice at that time of year. Here, I was able to contribute to Diane's delivery of the wow factor. She spoke to me, and I arranged for the wedding lunch to be held in our corporate dining room, a magnificent setting on the twenty-eighth floor overlooking the harbor, Sydney Harbor Bridge, and the opera house. We topped it all off with a wedding cake made by the bank chef, and the best Australian wine from our cellar.

This couple became loyal bank clients and advocates, investing a further $2 million and more and referring numerous other clients from Germany to our bank. And the marriage celebrant and her husband returned their more modest investments to the bank as well.

EVERY COMPANY AND every person has the opportunity to deliver amazing service that earns customer loyalty and referrals, builds the reputation and success of the company, and reflects well on the employee. Focusing employees on delivering this type of service is one of the most important things a leader can do. It just takes some attention to the tone and culture of the organization and some effort in training and developing employees.

YOUR NEW HEALTH REGIMEN

Work on building a culture that values customers by focusing your attention on customers and modeling customer care.

Make sure your operation and reward systems support superior customer assistance and experiences.

Understand your wow factors and let employees know how to leverage them.

Be sure your frontline employees have the skills to effectively deal with clients—recruit the best and train the rest.

Focus employees on turning emotionally charged moments into an exceptional experience.

Train employees to deliver exceptional service, never argue, be persistent, and develop advocates who refer friends and family.

Ensure that your teams understand customer lifetime value and empower them to make decisions to retain your loyal customers.

Measure customer connection regularly and use the measurements in your development plans.

Use various techniques for gathering information on customer connection.

When assessing customer connection results, aim for more than "satisfied" customers. You want delighted customers!

PRESCRIPTION 6

THE CURE FOR EMPLOYEES WHO AREN'T FOCUSED ON THE COMPANY'S GOALS

THERE'S A SIMPLE truth that all hold to in the world of strategy: He who executes best, wins. While creating a great strategy is . . . well . . . great, it won't get you very far if you aren't able to implement it and use it to build the success of your company. High-level leaders usually create strategy and develop overarching plans for implementing it, but it's the lower-level managers and front-line employees who are really responsible for the execution. So, if your employees are not dedicated to seeing the strategy succeed, it never will.

There are many reasons why employees may not be focused on the company's strategic goals. Poor strategy creation from above, lack of clear communication about the strategic goals, lack of connection between strategic goals and individual work and goals, and poor tracking of the company's progress toward the goals are the biggest factors. What this all boils down to is employees who aren't focused on the company's outcomes because they feel they have no input or stake in the direction of the company and are disconnected from the company mission.

To avoid this problem, leaders must ensure that everyone on the team knows the reasons behind the business strategy, is excited about that vision, can clearly see where the company is headed, and is personally involved in setting the intentions that need to be achieved.

Therefore, my sixth prescription is:

R_X *If you want to keep employees focused on company goals, create a sound strategy that will resonate with them, communicate about the strategy clearly and often, have a game plan linked to team and individual goals to implement the strategy, and track progress so that employees understand how they can help the company succeed.*

CREATE A STRATEGY THAT RESONATES WITH EMPLOYEES

In every leadership role, we must develop inspired but workable strategies. Strategies—clear courses of action that unify your workforce toward a single purpose—are powerful, particularly when you follow through with good implementation. It is a leader's responsibility to create a winning strategy that accurately defines how the organization will succeed, grow, prosper, and surpass the competition.

There are many different levels of strategy: strategies for floatations, listings, IPOs, restructures, implementing staff incentive schemes, lifting performance, product or service ideas, supplier selection process, and developing your people. The one constant is the critical steps in formulating and implementing a strategy.

To develop solid strategies, you must first "do the desk time," focusing intently on analyzing information, learning your market, ensuring that your products are meeting real market needs, and organizing and training your people. Once you have this foundation in place (which is not a simple process, but also is not the subject of this book), how do you go about determining an appropriate strategy for your organization or even your team? Following are some guidelines to use when assessing your strategic options.

Your strategy needs to be aligned with the organization's overarching mission or vision. For example, if part of your vision is to reduce adverse environmental or social impacts, you could aim at reducing ecological damage and work accidents. To optimize your effectiveness, you would not only reduce these negative outcomes but also search for ways to create a positive environmental outcome and ideas to create a happier, healthier, and more content workforce.

Many leaders become frustrated with the task when undertaking a time-consuming strategic planning process. Often this occurs because they have not looked into the future and involved all the key players in the process. To overcome this frustration, ensure that you look beyond the numbers. Identify long-term factors facing the business, and ensure that you have frank discussions with all key decision makers, including those who will be responsible for driving the implementation process.

- Build your strategy around the strength of your organization, employees, and customers.
- Consider long-term issues facing your business.
- Consider that a successful strategy should be bold, creative, and well thought out, with execution in mind. It also must

guide change, be easily communicated, and create commitment and passion, convincing people that its aims are worth
pursuing even when the going gets tough.

■ Review what your competitors are doing. Create strategies to
surpass them in the market.

■ Don't base your whole strategy on what your rivals are doing;
create some original pathways. Be inventive and drive the
industry with your leadership. A leader of an organization leads
into the future; she does not simply repeat what has already
been done.

■ Consider letting employees know that you are analyzing strategic
options or direction and invite their input. This is a great way to
support a culture of initiative and to create buy-in early on.

■ Set a clear path, but not a rigid one. Allow for alteration of the
strategy if necessary.

■ Keep it simple and focused. If it is too complicated and con-
voluted, employees will have a hard time understanding and
supporting it.

■ Inspire participation with your strategy—it should be exciting!

If you follow these guidelines when creating a strategy, you'll be
further down the road of ensuring employee support for the strategies you develop. Strategies require rigorous implementation planning and constant review, so the strategy development process needs
to account for this. A clearly defined strategy helps the communication, implementation, and measurement processes enormously. Your
end plan should include the following information:

■ Clear goals and objectives that capture precisely what you aim
to achieve

- Justification for the achievability of your strategic goals
  - Concise measures of performance and time frames for those measures
  - An established review schedule that compares daily, weekly, and monthly progress against the plan for the success of the strategy
  - A contingency plan and timetable for potential course adjustments

If your strategy development process does not account for all of these elements, you'll have a very difficult time explaining the strategy in concrete terms or implementing it in a way that earns the buy-in of all employees.

COMMUNICATE ABOUT STRATEGY CLEARLY AND OFTEN

Once you've created the best strategy for your organization, it's time to start letting everybody know about it. If employees don't know about or understand the strategic goals for the company, how can they possibly align their individual work and goals with the strategy? Leaders, from the head of the company to individual team leaders, must clearly articulate the strategic direction of the company to all employees, with passion. If you want your employees to contribute to the success of a given strategy, make sure to do the following in your communications:

- Before you begin, determine how best to explain the strategy. Talk to friends, colleagues, and subordinates about it and then ask, "If this strategy was communicated to you as an employee in a company, how would it make you feel? Would you feel a sense of trust in the leadership team? Would it inspire confidence? Is it reasonable? Does it make sense? Does it invoke your desire for success?" If the answer to any of these questions is no, find out why. It may be in the strategy or in how you are communicating it. Once you discover the weaknesses, make necessary changes.

■ Be clear, truthful, and transparent when describing how the strategy was created. This will build trust, respect, and a feeling that you have taken employees into your confidence and that you believe in their ability to comprehend higher-level planning.

■ Keep your people informed of what is happening in your industry. This will help them understand why your strategy looks like it does. They will grasp how the competitive marketplace affects corporate strategy and team business plans.

■ Communicate to all what they need to accomplish to have the company meet its objectives, presently and in the future. A clear picture and purpose will help your employees hold proposed activities against the vision and see if they will help your company get there. When an employee understands what

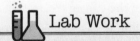 Lab Work

According to Robin Cohn, author of *The PR Crisis*, "Management is often so removed from employees that they don't have a sense for how something will be perceived, misunderstood or not understood" (Krell, 2006).

needs to be achieved, he will find it much easier to contribute. If everyone understands what needs to be done—why, when, and how—you will be surprised at how quickly the strategy is embraced and breeds success.

■ Make your initial communication the strongest and most inspiring. Keep fear of failure and intimidation out of your explanation. Instill a sense of strength and confidence through your delivery.

■ Sprinkle all company and team communications with language that relates back to the corporate or team strategy to keep it in the forefront of everyone's thinking. Be creative to arouse interest and inspire people to ask questions.

■ Discuss the plan as a guide rather than a rigid set of commandments so people are prepared to veer in other directions as needed. It's just as important for employees to be flexible and open as it is for leaders.

 *If you tell people the destination but not how to get*
there, you will be amazed at the results.

—GEORGE PATTON

IMPLEMENT YOUR STRATEGY CAREFULLY TO ACHIEVE BUY-IN

This is the longest section in this prescription because implementation (or execution) is typically where strategies fail and where the dedication of employees makes the biggest difference. The leader's role never ends with forming a strategy. Successful implementation requires strong leadership as well. A big part of that leadership is determining how to get individual employees to support the strategy through their actions and how to align the work of each individual with the strategic goals of the team and company. Remember, she who implements best, wins.

Following are some of the reasons why implementation is often more difficult than developing strategy:

- Many senior leaders believe their role is finished when strategy is in place. They are trained to plan and strategize and believe implementation is the domain of middle management.

- Strategy is set by a small number of people but implemented by a much larger group—the entire team of employees.

- The leaders of the business need to achieve the buy-in of all their teams' players, which can be difficult.

- To clearly communicate to the whole organization what needs to happen for the strategy to succeed, leaders need to address changes and requirements every day.

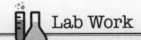 Lab Work

"According to conversations with business school faculty colleagues conducting research on companies based in Canada, Mexico, and the U.S., 70 percent to 90 percent of enterprises fail to successfully execute their strategies" (May, 2005).

To help you overcome these challenges, I've developed some general guidelines for implementation and some specific processes and tools that you can use in your organization.

The Seven Cs of Implementation

❶ Connecting

I have mentioned before how important it is for leaders to connect their heads to their hearts and the critical need for an authentic connection with others. This builds trust and respect because this approach displays honesty and provides the transparency that your employees, peers, and customers seek. This type of connection is vital, particularly during times of change, such as when a new strategic direction is being implemented. Never lose sight of the responsibility and integrity needed to maintain this approach. Once you have gained trust, resorting to coercion or manipulation will only result in disheartened employees and customers and a failed plan.

❷ Communicating

I've already addressed the importance of communication, but when you're implementing a strategy, communication is key. Leaders must constantly communicate the strategic direction—what has been done, what needs to be done, why it is being done, and where to get any necessary information. But in times of massive change, communicating every minor development or setback can create anxiety. You need to be the barometer of your team and assess what to communicate and the timing of these communications. Remember, though, to be honest. Don't lie to your team, even when things aren't necessarily going well. As you implement your plan, the process may reveal its weaknesses; keep communicating and informing employees as your path changes. Don't shy away from the emotions and fears this may evoke. Confront them head-on with compassion and understanding.

❸ Challenges

Having your team rise to a challenge and attain new heights is what leadership is all about. Prepare your team for challenges by hiring the right people for the right roles, developing their attributes and skills, building their self-esteem, and boldly leading them to become a winning team. Make it clear that you want them to strive for exceptional levels of performance, surpassing the goals set by the strategic plan, particularly if you have a high-performance team.

❹ Change Agents

Implementing a new strategy inevitably involves change across a wide spectrum of teams and activities, and change creates emotional upheaval. Many leaders, while comfortable with strategic issues and crunching the numbers, fall short in dealing with emotion. It is very important for these leaders to obtain professional guidance to address this situation. To be a successful change agent, a leader needs to show his authenticity, empathy, and compassion as his people grapple with change. Remember, successful business is all about feelings, so don't be afraid to address them. Issues will arise that cause changes in the plan. Be prepared to anticipate these and keep employees in the loop. Trust that they can handle the changes and they will. Place strong employee change agents in pivotal positions to help their peers deal with the ambiguity that may unfold.

❺ Customers

As you go about implementing your plan and navigating your way through the changes, remember to keep your customers foremost in your mind and remind all of your team members to do the same.

Continually put yourself in the customer's shoes and ask, How and why will this enhance the customer experience?

❻ Course Corrections

Although you need to start with a clear direction when you create a new strategy, you also need to be ready to navigate your way around obstacles. In tough, uncharted territories innovative ideas are the key to getting ahead, so involve your entire team in finding the gems that make a difference. You cannot change the wind's direction, but you can change the angle of your sails as you guide your team into the winner's circle. Correcting your course means learning from your mistakes and preempting disasters before they strike. This includes developing people and, when all else fails, releasing people who do not meet the team's standards. Let your team know that while the strategy is important and you are committed to achieving it, as they all should be, you are not blind to other possibilities or the need to alter course occasionally.

❼ Commitment

Commitment across the entire team is an absolute necessity to successfully implement a strategy. Each person's responsibility for achieving the team and company goals needs to be agreed on at the outset, and in writing. The leadership team needs a game plan (see next section) that the entire team knows and understands, one simple yet powerful enough to ensure that you achieve the intended results.

 There are two types of people—anchors and motors. You
want to lose the anchors and get with the motors because
the motors are going somewhere and they're having
more fun. The anchors will just drag you down.
—WYLAND, WORLD-RENOWNED MARINE ARTIST

CREATE A GAME PLAN

A strategic game plan sets the course for a team to meet its goals. It is a critical element in the implementation process, useful to any manager, regardless of level. The game plan also offers an important opportunity to create buy-in for the team's strategic goals and the strategic direction of the company. This plan will help employees learn how the strategy will be implemented through their team's activities and their individual goals.

I've created a sample game plan that will help you understand the level of appropriate detail and the type of information presented. Use the sample and the following guidelines to help you prepare your own game plans. You can prepare a game plan to achieve any outcome, internal or external. If you are managing a sales team, for instance, a game plan can be built around customer service, whole-process pipeline management, increasing revenue and performance management, or using the ideas in this book to tailor your own plan.

- Involve your team in setting the implementation game plan. The plan should succinctly cover what you need to do to achieve your business goals.

- Your game plan should be simple and focused and very clearly link to strategy. It should be clear to everyone that sticking to the game plan means achieving the business goals.

- The game plan should be memorable and easily communicated. Ideally, it will consist of about five key points that are communicated constantly, ensuring that everyone knows what you need to do.

- Use key performance indicators in the game plan to tie back to the key measurements of the company's goals, particularly financial measures such as revenue, sales, profit, etc. This is essential to ensure that following the game plan will achieve the desired results.

- When talking about the game plan, keep in mind that you must articulate five things:
    - You sincerely believe the right people are in the right roles.
    - Following the game plan will mean achieving team strategic goals.
    - Achieving team strategic goals will mean that corporate strategic goals can be achieved.
    - Every team member's input and effort is valuable and necessary to achieve the desired results.
    - You have total confidence in every team member's ability to meet expectations.

SAMPLE GAME PLAN

Strategic Theme: Create partnerships within the industry to drive referrals and increase business, thereby increasing revenue.

Team: Sales

❶ Establish some parameters for the types of partnerships the team could build that would be most beneficial to both parties. Partnerships should

- leverage both parties' strengths;
- represent mutual trust and benefit; and
- provide dynamic opportunities.

❷ Identify current customers or other entities who operate within the industry and with whom potential win-win partnerships could be formed. Then,

- leverage current partnerships;
- identify companies or organizations with common goals; and
- create interconnected networks.

❸ Create a list of key selling points that will help all team members convince influential customers that partnerships can be win-win. Team members might

- leverage the company's reputation in the industry;
- describe what the company can offer its partners;
- focus on partnership development in skills workshops and other development programs; and
- use right-brain thinking to become more intuitive, conceptual, and relational.

❹ Build nonbusiness connections that can develop into mutually beneficial relationships over time. Look for connections that will have synergy and be dynamic.

❺ Create relationships between clients to improve the company's reputation for interest in developing partnerships beneficial to its clients.

- Create a database that offers information about clients other than the usual information the company tracks.
- Constantly surprise clients by creating connections that exceed their expectations.

Align Team and Individual Goals with the Strategy

Once you've developed a game plan for achieving your team's goals, it is time to translate that game plan into individual goals for each team member. These goals are not dictated or imposed by the leader; rather, they are set collaboratively with the employee's input. When people participate in setting their goals and plans, their buy-in is enhanced, their attitudes are improved, and they will work harder to achieve the desired outcomes. Manipulation and coercion do not mix well with employees achieving their goals.

The key to successfully setting individual goals is a sharp focus, engendered by the leader, on setting clear, "smart" goals and outlining definitive actions to support them. There are five key characteristics that individual strategic plans/goals should hold to.

- **Specific:** What will be achieved? Who else is involved in or must contribute to achieving this goal?

- **Measurable:** How will progress or success be measured? Quantity, quality, number, financials, time? How will we know when the goal has been achieved?

- **Attainable:** Can the goal be achieved? Do we have control over the outcome? Does it have enough flexibility to recover from unexpected changes?

- **Relevant:** Does this goal support the team's strategic goals? The company's strategic goals? Does it tie in to the game plan?

- **Time Frame Oriented:** When does this need to be completed? When are the checkpoints?

Together, these criteria make a goal SMART: specific, measurable, attainable, relevant, and time frame oriented. Setting goals and achieving them are two totally different things, but if you set SMART positive goals, you can then create actions that will drive you to success. For instance, if you are trying to lose weight, you might say, "I aim to lose ten pounds by improving my eating habits and increasing my exercise." Is this a SMART positive goal? No!

A different way of phrasing the goal to make it specific, measurable, attainable, relevant, time frame oriented, and positive would be "I will lose one pound weekly over ten weeks, which will reduce me to my ideal weight. I will achieve this by increasing my intake of fruit to three pieces daily, having four vegetables with dinner, and reducing sugars, fats, and simple carbohydrates to less than 10 percent of my food intake. My exercise program will be thirty minutes of brisk walking or a thirty-minute workout in a gym five times weekly."

If you are a salesperson aiming to achieve six sales per week, you will set your goal knowing your pipeline success rate in locating prospects, obtaining interviews, and closing the sale. So, you might describe the goal as "I will do telephone prospecting two hours daily or until I have a minimum of twenty appointments set for the following week. If my closure rate on appointment to sale falls below my established 30 percent, I will work on my interviewing skills to bring my closure rate back to a minimum 30 percent. If my closure rate stays below 30 percent for two successive weeks, I will ask my manager to attend interviews with me to analyze my techniques and call prospects who did not accept to provide me with feedback. I will then take action to make the necessary adjustments and have my manager monitor my progress daily until I am consistently achieving my goal of six sales weekly."

When you and your employee have written the goals, check whether they meet the SMART positive criteria. Once the goals are set, reviewing them daily is critical and needs to become a ritual. Ask your employees to review their goals and visualize how they will feel on achieving the completed goal each morning, and then repeat the process each evening. This aligns the conscious and subconscious mind and inculcates the positive thoughts of attaining the goal.

An unwritten want is a wish, a dream, a never happen. The
day you put your goal in writing is the day it becomes a
commitment that will change your life. Are you ready?
—TOM HOPKINS, AUTHOR AND MOTIVATIONAL SPEAKER

When working with employees to set individual goals, leaders must remember that they are responsible for ensuring that everyone receives the necessary training in the skills needed to achieve their goals, if those skills are not already well developed. Don't forget that an employee may also have a set of personal goals that he is working toward as part of the development process. At individual and team development sessions, skills should be developed to parallel the requirements to keep their results on track. The development process must cohere to the strategy, or employees will feel pulled in multiple directions and it will be difficult for them to fully support the strategic direction of the company.

Develop Tools for Achieving Team and Individual Goals

Once you have your team game plan and each team member has a defined set of individual goals, the next step is to introduce tools that the team can use to help them achieve their goals.

The first tool I recommend is the Strategy for Goal Achievement form (see page 172). This form can be part of the game plan for the team or an individual exercise to help someone understand how to achieve her goals. On the form, you can list the obstacles you face in trying to achieve a certain goal and the strategies (keep them specific) that you'll use to overcome those obstacles. I've presented a sample form here, but it can take on any format you like. This tool will keep individuals very focused and thinking creatively about how to achieve their business results.

STRATEGY FOR GOAL ACHIEVEMENT	
Intention (Goal)	

Obstacles	**Strategies to Overcome Obstacles***
1.	1.
2.	2.
3.	3.
4.	4.
5.	5.

*Strategies become time-bounded "action items" in the weekly action plan.

Once the team members have each created a strategy for achieving their goals, you can move on to developing monthly and weekly action plans. As a leader, you can create one for your team so that you know what to look for in terms of weekly progress; you can even indicate who is responsible for each task on the weekly plan. Individuals can use it to guide their day-to-day activities. You may ask employees to send you their action plans with notes on progress at the end of each week and a new action plan for the following week. This will help you make sure that everybody is on course.

Using this tool, or something similar, will take no more than thirty minutes a week and will dramatically increase the chances of the team and each individual achieving their strategic goals.

Obviously, there are many similar tools you could create to track your team's progress. There are even software packages devoted to

---

WEEKLY ACTION PLAN

Week beginning _____

Critical Actions This Week

Action   **What Day**

_____   _____

_____   _____

_____   _____

_____   _____

_____   _____

Contacts to Make This Week

Name   **What Day**

_____   _____

_____   _____

_____   _____

---

this task. The key is for everybody in an organization and a team to use the same tools so that measurement of and communication about goal progress is easy for everyone.

TRACK YOUR PROGRESS

As I have mentioned, superior implementation starts with great strategy. But to ensure that a strategic direction continues to be relevant and feasible, leaders must conduct regular strategic reviews. The frequency of reviews depends on the complexity of the strategy and business results. Even if everything seems to be going well and to plan, a six-month strategic review should be conducted. The review can cover corporate strategy, business unit strategy, key performance indicators, game plans for individual business units and teams, communication of the strategic direction, and any updates that need to be shared.

Tracking the progress of a team or an individual toward key strategic goals should be a constant exercise. Otherwise it's impossible to know when a course correction is necessary. Evaluating all team members' progress against their goals on a daily, weekly, and monthly basis is essential to ensure they remain on track individually and as a team to achieve the company's outcomes. The process for tracking progress is the same as that presented in Prescription 4 on performance management:

- Daily monitoring of key activities
- Weekly monitoring of individual and team results
- Monthly monitoring of individual results via one-on-one meetings
- Monthly team results analyzed at leaders' meeting
- Quarterly reviews to determine if the strategic direction is still the correct fit and ensure the team is on track with results and people development

At each stage of this process, leaders should review employees' progress, adjust their actions, and share ideas and initiatives. Use the structured review processes and tools to make sure that progress tracking takes place at all levels. Communicate constantly. As soon as you leave employees in the dark, they will abandon the plan.

EVERY COMPANY AND every leader wants to see success in the market. They want more customers, greater revenue, increased growth, or some other measure of success. The only way to make this happen is to have all employees working toward the same set of goals, the same strategic direction. If employees aren't focused on the company's goals or the goals of their teams, the company won't achieve the success it desires.

 Do you want to be safe and good, or do you
want to take a chance and be great?

—JIMMY JOHNSON, DALLAS COWBOYS SUPER
BOWL–WINNING COACH, 1992 AND 1993

YOUR NEW HEALTH REGIMEN

Develop strategies that are bold, creative, well thought out, based on solid market and competitor research, and in line with the company's and employees' strengths.

Communicate about the strategy often and clearly.

Inspire trust and confidence through your strategy development and communication.

Implement your strategy carefully, as this is when most strategies fail.

Make sure all team and individual goals support the company's strategic direction.

Create a game plan for achieving team goals; involve your team in creating the plan.

Create individual targets that are specific, measurable, attainable, and relevant and that can be accomplished within a set time frame.

Work with all team members to set SMART positive goals.

Use planning tools to help teams and employees track their progress and achieve their goals.

Track the progress toward strategic targets on a corporate, a team, and an individual level.

PRESCRIPTION 7

THE CURE FOR MANAGERS
WHO CAN'T LEAD

"CONGRATULATIONS! WELCOME TO management!"

I remember hearing those words clearly when I was appointed to my first management position as regional sales manager of a team of fifteen salespeople. It was the same team that I had been a member of the previous day. My peer group had been very happy to see me promoted; they saw it as a win for the team.

Wow! How their attitude changed within a matter of weeks. There were a number of things they couldn't understand, including why I wouldn't share management secrets with them; why I insisted on performance standards higher than our previous boss; and why my relationship with them had changed.

 The secret to my success is that I bit off more than I
could chew and chewed as fast as I could.

—PAUL HOGAN, ACTOR WHO PORTRAYED CROCODILE DUNDEE

There were also things I had trouble understanding, such as why it didn't work when I barreled along expecting them to lift their performances dramatically overnight without any development from me. I had to learn a lot in those early days. It was during this time that it really hit me that leading people is all about feelings. This realization led me to become more compassionate, and to build trust and respect rather than demand improved performance.

It was during this time that I also learned who the most important leader for my team was. It wasn't our company CEO! In the eyes of a team, the most important leader is their boss. You are the CEO of your team. There is lots of evidence to support this fact. For instance, who was it at school who stood out the most for you as a student? The principal? No, it was your teacher. You can probably easily recall your best teacher and your worst teacher. Why? Because you judged them by the same criteria: how they made you feel.

The same criteria apply when you think of your best and worst bosses. The most important thing you can do as a new leader is to work at building relationships while operating from the heart, having compassion and empathy, and building trust and respect in a firm but fair way.

Authentic leaders inspire *followership* rather than seeking control. As a new leader, it is important to transform your thinking from "I" to "we." Only when thinking this way can you go about unleashing the power of the organization by developing people to achieve their optimum potential and transform their behaviors.

Many managers are in the same position I was, rising into management with little or no training on how to be a leader. This may be your own situation or the situation of some of the people who report to you. And some people have never had a good role model to emulate for leadership attitudes and abilities. But these limitations don't mean that we can't all become good leaders.

If you or someone you manage lacks good leadership skills, you had better address this problem immediately, because without these skills, it will be almost impossible to guide your team and company to success. As you may have gathered by now, if you aren't a strong leader, it's likely that your team won't respect you, will have bad attitudes, will be discontent, will underperform, and won't really care about customers or the company's goals. Remember what I said in the introduction about the four reasons why employees fail, and how these reasons all fall on the leader's shoulders? For a quick review, the four reasons are

- Poor selection at hiring time—our selection
- Poor skills left undeveloped—our coaching and development
- Poor attitude allowed to persist—our environment
- Poor leadership—our abilities

That's why my final prescription is:

R_X   If you want to lead a team to success
and achieve success yourself, you must
be dedicated to developing your and your
employees' leadership skills, building a culture
of strong leadership, finding and being a good
mentor, and reading and sharing this book.

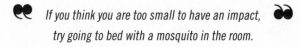

If you think you are too small to have an impact,
try going to bed with a mosquito in the room.

—ANITA RODDICK, FOUNDER OF THE BODY SHOP, ENVIRONMENTALIST

BE COMMITTED TO GREAT LEADERSHIP

Throughout this book, I've highlighted the attributes and skills of a good, authentic leader and how these attributes and skills can translate into a high-performing team and company. Following is a list of these attributes and how they contrast with the priorities of a managerial mind-set:

Leaders ...	Managers ...
Make informed, inspired decisions, even when the decisions are tough	Control processes
Set and explain clear expectations	Assume responsibility
Create new strategies and plan for their success and the success of their team	Manage within set guidelines
Inspire collaboration	Referee disputes
Model, promote, and reward initiative	Exert authority
Form and share vision and values	Solve problems
Build self-esteem and focus	Police behavior
Sponsor and support positive change	Minimize impact of change
Connect with people openly, honestly, and authentically to build relationships	Connect with people in an effort to lift bottom-line results
Develop people	Manage things

This list is not meant to minimize the importance of what managers do. Instead, it shows a pattern that helps better define authentic leadership and how authentic leadership can lead to higher levels of success. If you or your employees are acting as managers today, you can become authentic leaders by reshaping your goals and your approach. Take some time to really think about what being an authentic leader means to you. What can you do differently? What would you have your managers do differently? How will you change how you spend your time?

Many aspiring leaders have the skills and abilities to achieve great results, but they rely solely on those abilities and instincts to move their businesses forward. This is a limited perspective, however, and will offer limited success. Don't wait to change that perspective. We all know that in business, change occurs very rapidly, and now is the time for you to set a goal to learn how you can improve your authentic leadership skills.

 **Lab Work**

OnPoint Consulting, based in New York City, conducted a survey of U.S. managers and human resource professionals about their organizations' performance management system. Fewer than 40 percent indicated that their current performance management process helped build a high-performing culture or provide useful data for succession planning and leadership development initiatives. Jennifer Forgie, a managing partner at OnPoint, believes the flaw is in the attitude of the managers, not the evaluation methods (Laff, 2007).

I cannot overemphasize the importance of setting goals, having a positive, achievement-oriented attitude, and being totally focused on essential components of success in becoming a good leader—or in any other endeavor for that matter. Being authentic means operating from the heart. Using the wisdom of the heart will help you make sound judgment calls, especially related to people, and to be a truly successful leader, excellent assessment of people is imperative. Without a strong commitment to becoming an authentic leader, you'll be hard-pressed to achieve your goal. There are many supremely talented people who never find real success. But do you know of one supremely *focused* person who has not achieved her business and personal goals? What you have to ask yourself is "Do I want to rise to the top, or am I more comfortable in the average zone?" I call average "Cream of the Crap." If you want to achieve higher and higher levels of success, becoming a dedicated student of leadership skills will set you on that path.

DIAGNOSIS: INEFFECTIVE LEADERSHIP FROM ABOVE

What if you find yourself reporting to an ineffective leader? I see two options, one of which is to move on to another position. The second—a better alternative for most—is to develop the skill I call "leading up."

In essence, this consists of applying our principles of leadership in a slightly different way, with focus on

- building a professional relationship;

- being a good finder when it comes to your leader's strengths; and

- offering to become directly involved and apply your own strengths, without volunteering criticism.

Keep your leadership journey open-ended, do not set your sights too low, and strive to be better tomorrow than you are today, and the future will take care of itself.

For example, if you believe your leader is failing to track and interpret the numbers effectively, you could say, "I'm sure you're on top of this, but the numbers are really what I love, and where I believe I excel. Would you be open to a brief weekly meeting for me to share what I see in this area, and you can let me know if I'm on the right track?"

We could debate whether this approach is honest in every respect. But I think we could agree that it has a better chance of getting win-win results than complaints or head-on criticism. I think it also meets the standards on our checklist for decision making—especially in its potential to improve the situation for everyone involved.

BUILD A CULTURE OF STRONG LEADERSHIP

As with any other priority you want to establish within your organization (like valuing people or inspiring initiative), if you want to support your own efforts and those of your employees to become good leaders, you have to build a culture that promotes good leadership. Following are some guidelines based on the parameters for the good health of an organization I've presented so far:

- Hire or promote your leaders well. Make sure your leaders want to be leaders and have the right personalities for the role.

- Focus on leadership skills during development sessions.

- Model great leader behavior, skills, and attitude.

- Inspire collaboration and communication among leaders.
- Explore leadership issues as the root cause of underperforming teams.
- Focus on leadership skills during performance appraisals.
- Walk the talk on feelings and authentic leadership.
- Model passion and enthusiasm while minding your mood.
- Encourage your leaders to add value to their peers, praising their strengths and acknowledging their accomplishments.

This list reflects the point I made in Prescription 1 and the rest of the book: A clear focus on people engagement, and in this case leader development, is the best way to change the environment in and performance of your organization or team. Employee development and self-development are the two most important jobs of any leader. Almost every leader can improve his success and the success of his team by developing his core leadership skills, which will also improve the morale, motivation, and retention of all team members. Core leadership skills include the following:

- Creating employee development plans
- Coaching/mentoring/engaging
- Enhancing team morale
- Providing a motivating environment
- Having employee career conversations
- Setting goals and meeting them
- Performance management

Provide training in core skills for any leaders who report to you, and seek out training for yourself, particularly in any potential growth area.

Holding regular leadership meetings with leaders on your team creates the opportunity to focus on specific events that affect retention. For example, the loss of a valuable employee could be discussed in terms of how it could have been prevented by the leaders involved. If you are going to hold these meetings, be honest and dig deep and wide. It's the only way they will help grow the skills of leaders.

Smart with Heart Leadership

Yum! the world's largest restaurant company and owner of such eateries as KFC, Taco Bell, Pizza Hut, Long John Silver's, and A & W Restaurants, is an example of a company that drives a strong set of core values where leaders are encouraged to provide innovative awards. Chairman David Novak set the scene for these awards back in 1994. As the new president of KFC, he introduced the now-famous "Floppy Chicken Award." This fake chicken was presented to outstanding performers with a comment of their achievement written on the chicken. Each one was numbered like the collector's item it was. Novak also gave the recipient a hundred dollars because, as he put it, "You can't eat a rubber chicken!"

When Peter Hearl was promoted from U.S. president of Pizza Hut to chief operating and development officer for Yum! in 2006, he picked up the "Smart with Heart" approach to operations his predecessor, Greg Creed, had initiated. Peter had each Yum! restaurant brand try to clearly define what "smart" and "heart" truly meant within their businesses. Having the teams define their high-impact drivers and then putting clear measurement methods around them is one of the reasons for the success of Yum!

Hearl has since instigated a Smart with Heart award: a large, impressive, heart-shaped light globe with *Yum!* emblazoned across it. The award is presented to Yum! employees and associates around the world who epitomize Smart with Heart leadership.

This is a great example of promoting heart within a business and having everyone involved in determining what Smart with Heart means to them.

 The days of the Lone Ranger are over. Every organization
worth its salt now realizes that every person in every
position is called upon to lead, and lead well.

—TOM PETERS, AUTHOR AND MOTIVATIONAL SPEAKER

DIAGNOSIS: NARROW FOCUS

In today's ever-changing world, there is a need for a soft focus, just like in a speed sport. Focus has to be on everything and nothing at the same time. Gone are the days when an intent focus on one particular facet was fine. Now we still need to focus intently but remain ever aware of our surroundings, focusing our attention on a number of things at once. We need to learn to hold our focus, along with a diffuse focus. This approach of soft focus helps us to engage our heads and hearts at the same time. The head likes to focus intently on subjects, ideas, and problems. The heart has a more diffuse approach as it works in our feeling life of care, respect, inner strength, reverence, courage, and empathy. By invoking both types of focus, we can begin to feel what it is like to engage our heads and our hearts at the same time.

These attributes of the heart are part of our emotional intelligence. The more we use and experience these capabilities, the more we improve in them. And studies show that workers with a strong suit of emotional competencies are twice as likely to succeed.

FIND AND BE A GREAT MENTOR

Seeking help takes courage, but it's well worth the temporary blow it deals to your ego. Actively learning from the best mentor you can find is the most direct route to success in any endeavor. Modeling your own activities after those of a real person worth emulating truly works.

An example of the huge impact a mentoring relationship can have happened at First Direct, an online and telephone bank in the United Kingdom. A small group of newly hired employees met with a senior manager for a half hour each week to discuss any issues during the five-week training period. The call center reduced its turnover rate by 50 percent. The attrition rate fell from 30 percent to 17 percent, saving the company £915,000 in recruiting and training costs. The company has decided to implement the program across the organization (Phillips, 2007).

Of course, to learn from a mentor, first you have to find the right person, pursue the knowledge, and fully immerse yourself in the discipline it takes to grow and change. I'd like to illustrate the importance of that principle with this story about a high-performance individual who wanted to reach greater heights.

Tom had the ability, education, and track record to achieve outstanding results in his new role as CEO of a financial services company. In this role, he had tremendous power and responsibility. He supervised a dozen regional sales managers and a total sales force of more than two hundred.

Five months into his new position, the results were falling short of Tom's expectations. His organization was not even on track to achieve the 3 percent growth targeted for Tom's first twelve months as CEO. He felt at a loss to explain the problem, since he was passionate, worked hard, and was well liked by his direct reports.

At a weekend dinner party, Tom met Terry, a top financial planner at a rival financial services company, and the two hit it off right away. Tom was impressed not only by Terry's overall presentation and business knowledge but also by his expressed pride in his current organization. Naturally, Tom went into recruiting mode, offering Terry a six-month guaranteed income increase of 10 percent to join his company.

To Tom's surprise and disappointment, Terry was unwilling to seriously contemplate the offer or consider moving over to Tom's company. He said he was very flattered but that his current organization was achieving double-digit growth, and his sales were growing in excess of that. More importantly, he felt it was an exciting place to work: morale was high, and he had tremendous loyalty to his current CEO, Dan, whom he said had truly transformed and invigorated the business in just eighteen months.

Through a restless night, Tom kept returning to the possibility of contacting Dan, the CEO behind the business that was generating such great results and engendering such trust and loyalty from a top-producing employee. He delayed taking that risk, deciding to give his own methods, drive, and team more time to turn results around.

A month later, the turnaround simply hadn't occurred, and Tom sat in his office struggling with his dilemma. Results were tracking only 2 percent year-on-year growth, even though he'd never worked harder. It was time to make that call to Dan.

Tom was surprised to find Dan very receptive to meeting with him, and they arranged to have coffee a few days later. Although Tom was nervous at first, Dan—an exceptionally well-presented, fit, and friendly man about fifteen years his senior—was calm and agreeable. The meeting was going well up to the point when Dan asked, "Tom, what would you say are your three biggest challenges now that you've been in your CEO role for six months?"

When Tom hesitated, Dan put him at ease. He said, "Looking at you, I see myself a number of years ago as a newly appointed CEO. I was eager to impress but really struggling to find the right levers to pull to get the results the role demanded—let alone the outstanding results I expected. I learned by experience, picking up tips and good advice from leaders along the way, but today I realize I would have developed much faster with a good mentor. If I offer to help you that way, and at the end of this conversation we both feel we are compatible, would you consider making this a regular meeting for that purpose?"

Tom agreed, and accepted the task of bringing those three major challenges to the table for his next meeting with Dan. He began thinking through which of his challenges needed the most attention. The first was obvious: his organization's unsatisfactory sales results. The second, he felt certain, was the challenge of recruiting top performers, although he also had frequent concerns involving strategic vision and values, enhancing the customer experience, and managing expenses. He settled on sales growth, recruiting top performers, and enhancing motivation and morale.

Although Dan saw the validity of Tom's nominated challenges, his response was a bit surprising. The crux of his response was "Let's really start with the basics, because there are many issues within each of these challenges. To become a true leader and approach your desired results, I believe it's critical to be methodical not only in what you do, but how, when, and why you do it. As we progress, you will gain a much stronger sense of what those important levers are and when to pull the ones that truly make a difference."

Over the next three months, Dan and Tom met regularly to discuss the current situation, and Dan was always ready to subtly weave in another leadership lesson. Tom was a diligent student, and he took the lessons back to the workplace. In no time he was engendering respect from his team and his superiors.

Dan introduced Tom to a proven way to improve results, along with a means of gaining the confidence to take fast, meaningful action. Overcoming his ego and inhibitions to seek advice was already opening new doors for Tom, and his future looked bright and filled with possibility.

READ, REREAD, AND SHARE THIS BOOK

Can this book help you become a highly successful leader? I believe, in my heart and head, that it can do just that *if* you truly commit to that goal. Even more important, I believe you can become successful and be authentic, consistently creating win-win scenarios for you and the people you lead. Again, this is true only if you are intent on learning new techniques and applying them.

Whether you use this book as a guide, find a mentor, or read every book on the market about leadership, I hope you work hard to improve your skills as a leader and the skills of your team members. Without great leadership, your team and organization will be average at best. Great leadership is the best way to engage people and ensure that everybody succeeds.

YOUR NEW HEALTH REGIMEN

Commit to becoming an authentic leader; be focused and dedicated to that goal.

Diligently work on your leadership skills on a daily basis.

Develop a culture focused on valuing good leadership and leadership skill development.

Find a leadership mentor and be one yourself.

Become a master of engagement. Work at engaging employees, customers, peers, and bosses!

And remember . . . it's all about feelings!

REFERENCES

Bielaszka-DuVernay, C. "Are You Using Recognition Effectively?" *Harvard Management Update* 12, no. 5 (May 2007): 2–3. Retrieved on June 13, 2007, from MasterFile Premier database.

Childre, D., H. Martin, and D. Beech. *The Heartmath Solution*. (San Francisco: HarpersSanFrancisco, 1999).

Durett, J. "R-e-s-p-e-c-t." *Training* 43, no. 6 (June 2006): 12. Retrieved on May 15, 2007, from Business Source Alumni Edition database.

Gallup Study: Engaged Employees Inspire Company Innovation. *Gallup Management Journal* (June 2006). http://gmj.gallup.com/content/24880/Gallup-Study-Engaged-Employees-Inspire-Company.aspx.

"How to Get and Keep the Best Employees." *HR Focus* 83, no. 12 (Dec. 2006): 10–15. Retrieved on June 12, 2007, from MasterFile Premier database.

Krell, E. "Companywide Trust Affects Productivity, Profitability." *New Mexico Business Journal* 30, no. 10 (Oct. 2006): 33. Retrieved on May 11, 2007, from MasterFile Premier database.

———. "Do They Trust You?" *HR Magazine* 51, no. 6 (June 2006): 59–65. Retrieved on May 11, 2007, from MasterFile Premier database.

———. "The Unintended Word." *HR Magazine* 51, no. 8 (Aug. 2006): 50–54. Retrieved on June 14, 2007, from MasterFile Premier database.

Laff, M. "Performance Management Gives a Shaky Performance." *Training & Development* 61, no. 9 (Sept. 2007): 18. Retrieved on September 28, 2007, at MasterFile Premier database.

Laposky, J. "Consumers Will Pay More for Good Customer Service: Study." *TWICE: This Week in Consumer Electronics* 19, no. 1 (2004): 82. Retrieved May 15, 2007, from the Academic Search Premier database.

Larkan, T., and S. Larkin. "Mission Impossible: Increasing Employee Trust in Your CEO." *Communication World* 23, no. 1 (Jan.–Feb. 2006): 40–41. Retrieved on May 11, 2007, from Business Source Elite database.

Leboeuf, M. *Greatest Leadership Principles in the World*. (1985).

———. *Things That Get Rewarded Get Done* (April 2003). [He states it as The Greatest Leadership Principle. "People do what you reward."]

Marr, J. W. "Latest Loyalty Report Further Demonstrates ROI of Customer Loyalty." Untitled monthly report on creating loyalty, Walker Info (May 2005). Retrieved on May 16, 2007, from www.walkerinfo.com/what/loyaltyreports/.

May, T. A. "Companies Striking Out on Strategy." *Computerworld* 39, no. 23 (June 2005): 21. Retrieved on June 19, 2007, from MasterFile Premier database.

McManus, K. "The Leadership Gap." *Industrial Engineer* 37, no. 5 (May 2005): 20. Retrieved on May 15, 2007, from Academic Search Alumni Edition database.

McNulty, E. J. "It's Time to Rethink What You Think You Know About Managing People." *Harvard Management Update* 11, no. 2 (Feb. 2006): 3–5. Retrieved on April 3, 2007, from Business Source Elite database.

Oakes, K. "Performance Management Lacks Consistency." *Training & Development* 61, no. 4 (Apr. 2007): 50-53. Retrieved on June 22, 2007, from MasterFile Premier database.

"100 Best Companies to Work for 2007." *Fortune*. Retrieved on June 14, 2007, from money.cnn.com/magazines/fortune/bestcompanies/2007/.

"Performance Management: Still a Long Way to Go for Many Companies." *HR Focus* 84, no. 10 (Oct. 2007): 8. Retrieved on September 28, 2007, at MasterFile Premier database.

Phillips, L. "Mentors Save First Direct £1m." *People Management* 13, no. 4 (Feb. 2007). Retrieved on May 11, 2007, from MasterFile Premier database.

Russel, D. "How Much Are Your Employees Costing You?—Tips to Improve Your Management Style and Increase Your Bottom Line." *Varibusiness Media* 58 (Dec. 5, 2005). Retrieved on May 15, 2007, from LexisNexis database.

Schneider, B. "Customer Satisfaction." *Leadership Excellence* 23, no. 8 (Aug. 2006): 13. Retrieved on May 15, 2007, from Business Source Premier database.

Sirota, D., L. A. Mischkind, & M. I. Meltzer. *The Enthusiastic Employee.* (Durett, 2006).

"Talent Management Among Top Priorities in 2005." *Business Journal (Central New York)* 19, no. 4 (Jan. 28, 2005): 14. Retrieved on June 13, 2007, from MasterFile Premier database.

Taylor, R. "Tackling Toxic Leaders." *Director* 60, no. 10 (May 2007): 27. Retrieved on June 13, 2007, from MasterFile Premier database.

"Top Tools for Motivation." *Incentive* 179, no. 11 (Nov. 2005). Retrieved on June 13, 2007, from MasterFile Premier database.

"Worker Myths Companies Accept." *Training & Development* 59, no. 7 (July 2005): 16. Retrieved on May 15, 2007, from Academic Search Alumni Edition database.

INDEX

House Calls Available

"Engaged People Deliver Exceptional Results"

Bring in Ken Wright from Engage4Results Pty. Ltd. for in-depth consulting, coaching and training in the following areas:

- Leadership
- Employee Engagement
- Emotional Intelligence
- Productivity Enhancement

You will receive a no-obligation initial meeting with your executives to tailor a specific program that is guaranteed to meet or exceed your needs.

That's our specialty . . . tailor-made programs guaranteed to succeed!

For further information and details contact:

www.Engage4Results.com

The Wright Program™
Develop ROE—Return on Engagement

Create your own "People Engagement Culture" to develop your team's authenticity, which will lift people's self-esteem, ignite team spirit, improve morale, engender trust, and propel results—all while having FUN! In short, you learn the "Rules of Engagement."

The Wright Program simplifies putting *The People Pill* into action and comprises the following package put together by Ken Wright and his wife Amanda Gore, an internationally recognized speaker on communication, EQ, and leading from the heart.

PACKAGE

- Facilitation Guide for Leader
- Journal for participants
- Instructional DVDs
- Copy of *The People Pill*
- As well as some exciting Leadership Enhancement products!

For more information and to order, visit:
www.Engage4Results.com
www.amandagore.com